THE MODERN CRAFT

EDITED BY
CLAIRE ASKEW *and* **ALICE TARBUCK**

THE
MODERN
CRAFT

POWERFUL VOICES
ON WITCHCRAFT ETHICS

WATKINS
Sharing Wisdom Since
1893

The Modern Craft

Edited by Claire Askew and
Alice Tarbuck

First published in the UK and USA
in 2022 by Watkins, an imprint of
Watkins Media Limited
Unit 11, Shepperton House,
83–93 Shepperton Road
London N1 3DF

enquiries@watkinspublishing.com

Commissioning Editor: Ella Chappell
Assistant Editor: Brittany Willis
Head of Design: Karen Smith
Production: Uzma Taj

A CIP record for this book is available
from the British Library

ISBN: 978-1-78678-644-9
10 9 8 7 6 5 4 3 2 1

Printed in the United Kingdom by
TJ Books

www.watkinspublishing.com

CONTENTS

Introduction — **08**

1 Witches and Wordsmiths, Sorcerers and Storytellers
By Iona Lee — **16**

2 Brass Knuckles, Broken Mirrors, Binders and
Glitter Bombs: *Empowerment, self-acceptance and
activism for queer working-class witches*
By Jane Claire Bradley — **26**

3 Altars of Transition
By Harry Josephine Giles — **40**

4 Mental Health and Magic:
On forging a path through the darkness, together
By Lisa Marie Basile — **56**

5 Polite Persecution:
Raising non-binary children, dismantling everything else
By Stella Hervey Birrell — **68**

6 Witch Boys and Devils on the Road:
The magic of troubled masculinity
By AW Earl — **78**

7 The First Rule of Witch Club
By Sabrina Scott — **94**

8   Witchcraft, Indigenous Religion and the Ethics of
Decolonization: *An experiment in co-labouring*
By Simone Kotva — **110**

9   Ethics and the World of African Traditional Religions
By Lilith Dorsey — **126**

10   Witchcraft in the Anthropocene
By Alice Tarbuck — **136**

11   A New Malleus Maleficarum:
The myth of the gender critical witch hunt
By Claire Askew — **150**

12   "What Are You Fighting?":
*Gender, witchcraft and the High Priestess from
one nonbinary witch's perspective*
By Em Still — **166**

13   You Cannot Heal Others Until you Heal Your Own
"Stuff": *A reflection on Hindu archetypes and self-healing
through ThetaHealing®*
By Briana Pegado — **180**

14   Giants, Weavers and Other Bodies
By Megan Rudden — **196**

15   Building a Cosmology of Access:
A day in the life of a disabled land-based practice
By Madelyn Burnhope — **212**

About the Contributors — 228
Acknowledgements — 237

INTRODUCTION

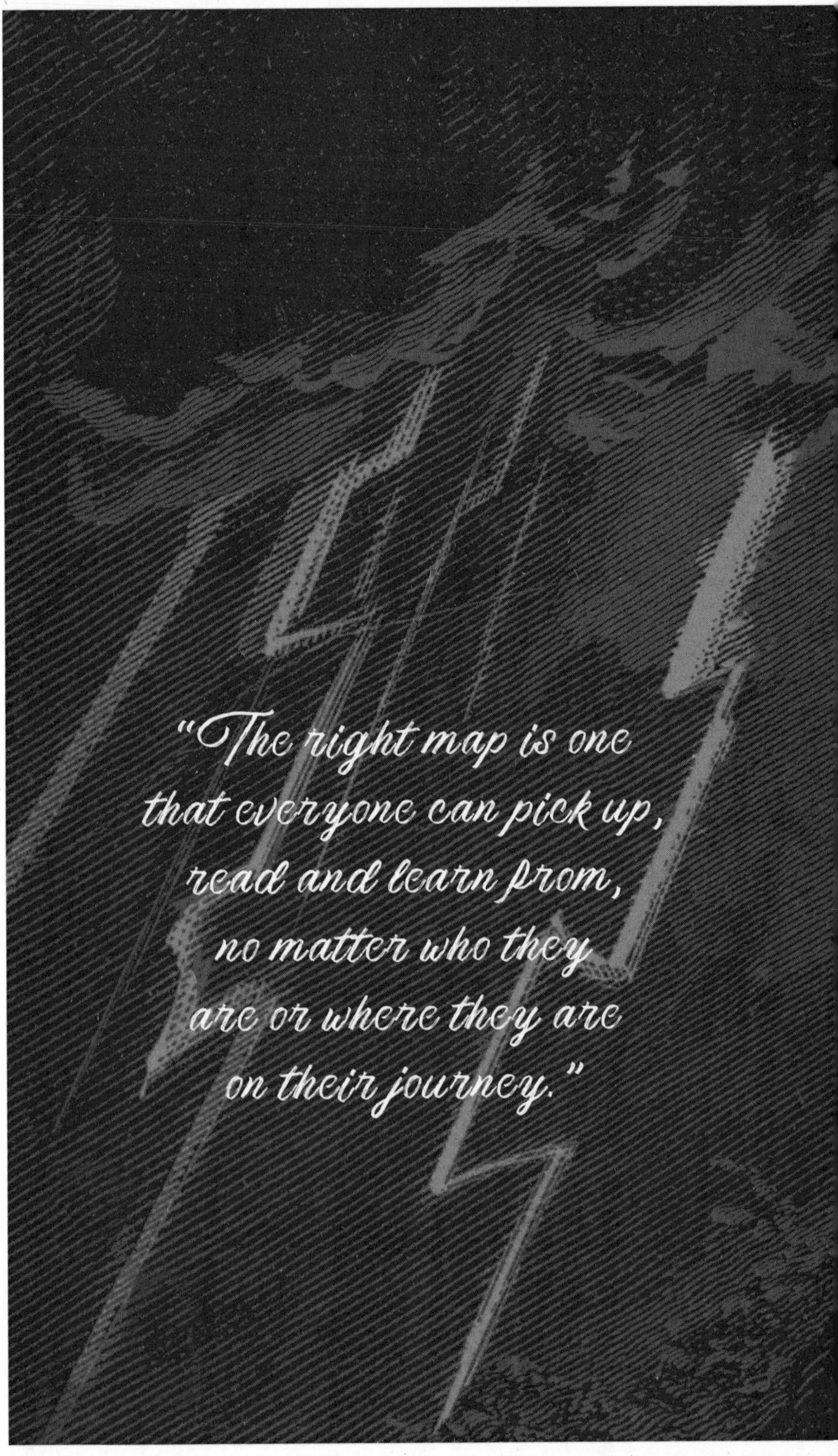

"The right map is one
that everyone can pick up,
read and learn from,
no matter who they
are or where they are
on their journey."

INTRODUCTION

BY CLAIRE ASKEW AND ALICE TARBUCK

s witches who grew up in the late 1990s and early 2000s – raised by *Hocus Pocus*, *Buffy* and *The Craft*, proficient in social media, dabbling from a young age in social justice – we both found ourselves longing, at times, for a handy manual on the ethics of setting up a witchcraft practice. Transforming from teenage goths who wore a lot of purple into fully-fledged, intersectional witches required finding answers to a great many questions: what is okay to include in my ritual practice, and what doesn't belong to me? How do I move beyond the gender essentialism that is so commonplace in occult iconography and language? How do I resist the lure of capitalism and its many cute-but-mass-produced witchy accoutrements? How do I work in a way that honours the land and acknowledges our state of climate crisis? How do I – how does any of us – develop a responsible witchcraft?

We'd long been grappling with these questions privately, but didn't voice them with each other until the day that Claire happened across what we now refer to as The Egg Post. The witchy corridors of blogging platform Tumblr – sometimes called "#witchblr" – are full of witches young and old, experienced and not so experienced, sharing instructions for spells they've completed and feedback on the results of those spells. Among these blogposts, Claire found a baby witch (that's witchblr code for a new practitioner) lamenting the poor results of a ritual performed using a chicken egg.

Egg rituals of the kind the Tumblr post described originated in Mesoamerican shamanism. The original ritual – named *la limpía* – sees the shaman summon negative energy out of the body of the subject and into the sealed capsule of a raw, unbroken egg. Though the ritual almost certainly began as part of a closed practice, which could only be performed by initiated individuals, "egg cleansing" has become commonplace in occult communities, with practitioners co-opting elements of the original ritual and tweaking it to fit their requirements. On witchblr and in other contemporary witchcraft spaces, you'll find examples of egg cleansing rituals that involve rolling the egg over the body of the subject, writing one's negative thoughts on the shell of the egg in marker pen, or sending one's anger at a person or situation into the egg by sitting it in front of you and then shouting at it.

What just about every egg-cleansing ritual has in common, however, is the final step: once the egg has absorbed the negativity that the subject wishes to let go of, it is usually either buried or taken to an open space and smashed. The negativity is thus banished from the person and given to the wider universe to deal with. What fascinated and horrified us about The Egg Post, however, was the baby witch's decision to keep and use the egg for non-magic purposes once the ritual was over. Namely, she had opted to cook and eat this capsule of negativity to avoid what she saw as the waste of a perfectly decent egg. This seemed, to us, like a very obvious example of auto-hexing. No wonder the poor wee witch subsequently took to Tumblr to complain that the spell did not seem to have been effective.

What began as aghast bemusement over The Egg Post transformed into an ongoing conversation that the two us have now kept up for several years. "We all really need a manual on this stuff," we'd regularly say to one another.

After all, how is the baby witch to know whether or not a spell is culturally appropriate when, as Simone Kotva points out in her essay on the ethics of decolonization: "like Western occultism in general, modern witchcraft in particular has been criticized for fostering an explorer's or collector's mentality – a hallmark of the very neo-colonialism its advocates so often purport to resist."

How are they to learn to make spells of their own when access to materials and resources is so often a barrier to new practitioners? "How do you learn about this?" Jane Claire Bradley asks in her essay on witchcraft, class and queerness. "Where do you get the books? The materials? And what if you can't afford it?"

Witchcraft is, after all – as Harry Josephine Giles elegantly puts it –"a muddy track running underneath the powerlines." How do we find that track and navigate it, especially as minority witches struggling against misogyny, homophobia, transphobia, racism, ableism and classism, all of which are baked into occult communities and larger institutions alike? AW Earl, in their essay on witchcraft and masculinities, says of magic: "It's about passion, about knack – sniffing the wind and tasting rain, trick shots taken with no formal study of calculus, knowing in the minute tensile shifts felt beneath your fingers when the dough has been kneaded enough. It is a craft that can be grown untaught, or passed from hand to hand – not merely learned."

How does anyone – let alone those who face additional barriers to access – make their way into such territory? That is the question we hope that *The Modern Craft* begins to answer. It is a collection of essays – some highly personal, others more academic – that together create a rich, provocative, practical, but by no means exhaustive map of this complex and ever-shifting terrain. In selecting contributors for this book, we prioritized the voices of minority practitioners with lived experience of working at intersections: folk we felt could best illuminate – as Lisa Marie Basile puts it – "what exists in the cracks that don't get much light." (Late on in the process of compiling these essays, we realized that the one voice we had particularly overlooked was that of the cishet man – we hope you'll forgive us for this omission, and suspect that readers seeking this particular viewpoint won't struggle to find it represented elsewhere in occult literature.)

With the right map, Madelyn Burnhope writes, "we can journey anywhere." The right map is one that everyone can pick up, read and learn from, no matter who they are or where they are on their journey. That's what we hope we have provided with *The Modern Craft*: an accessible and illuminating tool for those who are – Madelyn again – "doing the magic of symbolic meaning-making."

Drs Claire Askew
& Alice Tarbuck

"How does anyone – let alone those who face additional barriers to access – make their way into such territory?"

WITCHES AND WORDSMITHS, SORCERERS AND STORYTELLERS

*"... all words have
the potential to be
magical ..."*

1

WITCHES AND WORDSMITHS, SORCERERS AND STORYTELLERS

BY IONA LEE

*W*ords conjure what is not there. Words can be weapons or tools. They can terrify or pacify, please or disgust, influence and alter.

As a wand conveys a spell, a word brings with it feeling, meaning, abstraction and history. A tyrant will cast chaos with his oratory. A storyteller will move with rhyme, rhetoric and rhythm. A salesman will mystify with jargon.

Words are immensely powerful, but we comprehend that it is not the words themselves that hold the power – they are not vessels – but rather symbols that channel meaning.

In the past, however, people have believed – and in some contexts, still do – that power resides in the words themselves: that certain words are magical in essence. Or, indeed, that all words have the potential to be magical: that language is magical in essence.

I am going to attempt to show you that magic and language are historically and inextricably intertwined, like the double helix of our DNA. They are two sides of the same enchanted coin, spinning in infinity. Whether one believes in magic, or simply in the emotional weight that can be afforded to language, magical language nonetheless exists and can be used to give and take power.

Before we go any further, I want to present you with two powerful words that may not be familiar to you. I think they will be useful in helping to unlock insight into the ways we perceive reality, and how that can be fluid.

The first is "emic". An emic understanding is an understanding of something within the context of its time or culture. An "etic" understanding is an understanding of something from the context of today – looking from the outside in. Think of them as being like the difference between empathy and sympathy.

One's perception of reality can shift, just as the shafts of sunlight between trees illuminate and refocus. It depends on your standpoint.

So then, magic, for our purposes, is an etic understanding of an emic reality.

Magic has been transmogrified by time and has journeyed through a forest of a thousand interlacing corridors to find itself subsumed by endless definitions and explanations: inspiration, weather, hallucination, gravity, power.

It does not matter if we do not believe in the reality of magic today. Simply put, our semantic realities have changed. What we once called alchemy has become chemistry. There was once no appreciable distinction between astrology and astronomy, nor glamour and grammar. Electrickery has become electricity.

"One's perception of reality can shift"

These processes remain mysterious: the layman can now call the lighting of a match a work of science, but probably does not fully comprehend the process, nor indeed, the reason for the flame.

The same is true of the powers of speech and language – we know that stories can affect us, we know that insults can offend us, we know that proverbs can reassure us, but not many of us can easily explain why. And that is okay – I am not a philosopher of language or a scholar of the science of linguistics. I am but a mere poet, dealing in metaphor and double meaning; explanation through abstraction; the beauty and the truth that lie in ambiguity.

Language and magic are pleasingly elusive and one could only pin them down with sky nails – but that doesn't mean that their use doesn't have consequences. It may sound fantastical to suggest that words can take on material form and effect tangible change, but what then is a promise doing, or an apology? What of the warning? Or the wedding vow?

It is perhaps difficult for the modern mind to appreciate the physical power that language will have possessed for the pre-literate people of pre-industrial Europe. The spoken word was a formidable force. Whether a prayer, the swearing of an oath or a magical incantation, speech was believed to manipulate the physical world.

Perhaps the most famous magical phrase, "abracadabra", is thought by some to translate to "I create as I speak". "Hocus-pocus" may translate to "this is my body".

In fact, etymology is one particular sun beam that can highlight language's gnarled roots in magic. Think of words like "curse" or "charm". The meanings of these words have wandered down two separate woodland paths. We still understand "charm" to be a magic spell, but it has also come to signify a means by which one might gain another person's liking. The double meanings of these words are at once literal and metaphorical.

Science has explained a great deal of what was once perceived to be supernatural; but, if you were to charm someone today, the result might very well be the same as if you had used magic.

This dichotomy is true of many words that are still in use. "Glamour" is a variant of the Scots word "gramarye", meaning a spell. Both come from the English word "grammar", which itself once meant magic, but now we understand it to be the rules governing the structure and composition of language. The way one constructs one's statements influences people, and this influence has, at times, been perceived to be magical.

This is true of the word "spell" itself. A spell is an incantation with occult power, but it is also how we form words with letters.

So we have established that both magic and language are powerful and have, at times, been understood in an emic sense to be one and the same. They can also, in an etic sense, be understood as metaphors or mirrors, for one another.

This is important, as well as interesting – but why? To answer that, we must first ask: what does magic do? It interferes with the perceived "natural" order of things.

A pervasive fear of the "wild wood" exists throughout folklore and literature. Psychologists have interpreted the trope of journeying into the forest as a metaphorical journey into the mind – the forest is our subconscious. The sometime friend and frequent foe often found within the forest is the witch; she lives in a house in the glade within our collective subconscious.

What is a witch? The witch is a universal archetype. The witch is a practitioner of witchcraft.

She is also an insult, an oracle, a midwife, a myth, a crime, a practitioner of religion, a sex symbol, a crone, a healer, a hag, a mother, a maiden, a goddess and a wise old woman. She repulses and seduces. She heals and harms. She brings life into this world and destroys it. She is order and chaos. She gives birth to the moon and she eats the sun.

The changeable nature of the witch is a reflection of the unpredictable and complex nature of us all. But, she is a woman. She is what is un-human about the human experience. We are not accustomed, from either a literary or a social-historical standpoint, to the idea of a woman's character being permitted to be complex.

The lack of power historically afforded to women has tended to make them be seen as one-dimensional, and this has been reflected in our narratives, stories and media. The witch represents our humanity, but we deny her her own humanity, as she is multi-dimensional and, therefore, monstrous.

The binary of gender was until recently generally taken for granted, and the apparent polarities of man and woman and good and evil seem to have aligned, so that the "mysteries" of womanhood became intertwined with the mysteries of witchcraft. To name something is hopefully to attempt to understand it, but a name confines as much as it defines. Our understanding of what the word "woman" means is, itself, evolving.

I believe that at the root of almost all accusations of witchcraft was a concern with the words, language and stories of women, and the power and influence that a skilful use of language might afford them. There is a historic distrust of women who are good with language or who claim a public voice, and we must learn from history. The witch trials of Europe and the New World were, in an emic sense, an attempt to silence the spells of witches – but we might understand them in an etic sense as a policing of women's speech. The witch may be considered a woman, but what is far more important to me is that she was a wordsmith. As Christina Larner says, "she has the power of words".[1]

A wise person would possess an extensive vocabulary. She would know the names of the plants and herbs that were best for healing. She would learn the names of the stars and constellations. She would memorize folk tales and perhaps the names of the spirits that lived in the old, contorted trees, the wishing wells and thresholds. Many extant spells rhyme or use repetition. Just as in literature, the rhetorical devices used in magical speech resonate powerfully, like a rhyming couplet winks the curtains closed. The witch plays with language to make her spells more powerful.

Historically, and in many cases currently, women have been excluded from power by male institutions. The world of word-smithery is an area in which power has been available to women. A curse, a spell, a muttering under the breath were things to which a woman could resort in opposition to male primacy. This adds to the stereotype of women as underhand and possessed of "slippery tongues": if one truly believed in the

---

1 Larner, Christina, *Witchcraft and Religion: The Politics of Popular Belief,* Ed. Alan MacFarlane, Basil Blackwell, 1984, p84

potential harm that words could cause, and if words were often the only resort for a woman given her lack of autonomy, then it would make sense to be wary of the words of women.

"The witch is not simply a creation of the patriarchy"

The existence of such things as the Scold's Bridle are testament to a masculine concern with what women might say and how they might say it.

Additionally, women may have turned to cursing to bring colour to their domestic existence. Witchcraft represents another way. It is excitement, rebellion, mischief and autonomy. The witch is not simply a creation of the patriarchy; women have invested in the character as a fantasy that allowed them to express taboos, unacceptable desires and revolutionary ideas.

It is believed that many women killed during the witch trials were in fact storytellers with linguistic and narrative skill evident in their confessions. If this were true, it would imply that some witches were persecuted not for their use of wicked magic, but for their daring to engage with the gifts of knowledge and language.

Storytelling can be a way of imparting wisdom – and just like ideas or experts, wisdom is often viewed with suspicion in times of social change. At times we have burned witches; other times we have burned books.

The most powerful in a society police the language of the oppressed. A woman's failure to control her tongue seems to have been the root cause of many accusations of witchcraft. A witch's words were her weapons. A witch's words were the only weapons she had to rail against authority.

As Malala Yousafzai wrote in her book *I Am Malala*: "Let us pick up our books and our pens ... they are our most powerful weapons".[2]

---

2 Yousafzai, Malala, "Malala Yousafzai: 'Our books and our pens are the most powerful weapons'", *The Guardian*, 12 July 2013

We must arm ourselves with the powers of language; name the things that we wish to understand; voice those words that intimidate, that seem a Pandora's box of malevolent power. By speaking these truths out loud, we harness this power, and if spoken enough they will turn to love spells muttered underneath the breath.

History can seem to have established a normality that is in fact not necessarily "normal" at all. We are so used to men as leaders, as storytellers, as speakers that society has often identified them as naturally better suited to these roles. However, women have been too often denied the opportunity to prove this assumption incorrect.

The witch trials have become a paradigm of the way in which society, even the state, has punished the oppressed for attempting to utilize one of the few powers generally available to them. Thankfully, things have got better for most women during the past four centuries, but women still remain oppressed to a degree; and they are by no means the only oppressed group.

By telling our stories, we can perhaps redress the imbalance in the normalization of our experiences. Stories are an insight into the inner lives of those other than ourselves. It is through stories that we can understand and empathize. It is through writing that one makes sense of something. Poems are puzzles to solve. Storytelling is humanizing.

The witch is a woman, perhaps, but women are not witches. They are humans who have long been misunderstood, for they have been unable to speak for themselves.

BRASS KNUCKLES, BROKEN MIRRORS, BINDERS AND GLITTER BOMBS

"My self-trust, courage and sense of connection to nature, magick and community have all increased exponentially as I've explored my own witchcraft path and practice."

2

BRASS KNUCKLES, BROKEN MIRRORS, BINDERS AND GLITTER BOMBS: EMPOWERMENT, SELF-ACCEPTANCE AND ACTIVISM FOR QUEER WORKING-CLASS WITCHES

BY JANE CLAIRE BRADLEY

*O*n the 1960s, the feminist collective Women's International Terrorist Conspiracy from Hell (W.I.T.C.H.), wore classic black witchy cloaks and pointy hats to drive news coverage and visibility of their protests. Combining performance art, protest and magic, they marched down Wall Street, hexed the financial district, gained worldwide media attention and sparked a series of spin-off collectives and actions across the United States. More recently, witches across the globe have joined forces in protest and spellwork for social justice, including casting mass hexes on rapist Brock Turner[1] and Donald Trump[2]. On the eve of Biden's inauguration, Reclaiming co-founder Starhawk led an online ritual to spin a web of protection over those involved.

---

1 www.vice.com/en/article/ywmzbw/hundreds-witches-hex-spell-stanford-rapist-brock-turner
2 www.wired.com/story/trump-witches/

There's commonalities between these: they gain attention for their causes (even as witchcraft moves toward mainstream visibility and acceptance, the media still loves to sensationalize it); they create impact, both magickal and mundane; they connect people, creating a sense of community and collective momentum; and for those involved, they create a sense of personal agency and empowerment in the face of oppressive circumstances and structures that might otherwise legitimately lead to a sense of intimidation, overwhelm, powerlessness and grief.

There's a rich historical and contemporary evidence bank for witchcraft being employed on a collective scale as a tool for social justice, change and empowerment. But mass actions don't emerge from a vacuum, and that makes me curious about the other acts of everyday magick not making headlines – in particular, the ones being performed by people experiencing marginalization within those same oppressive systems and structures. Bringing in my own heritage and identity – queer, mixed-race, working-class, brought up in poverty – I'm continually fascinated by the ways people with these sorts of backgrounds and experiences explore and access protection, justice and power, for themselves and their communities. As a teenager on a notoriously unsafe council estate, my earliest dabblings in witchcraft were invisibility spells to protect me on my walk home from school. Having experienced homelessness and displacement at an early age, creating small makeshift altars in significant places was a way to orient and build relationships with my environment. As queer kids in my best mate's tower-block bedroom, teaching ourselves tarot felt like a key to the future: a way to imagine what might be waiting for us, and whether it was worth holding on for. As legendary non-binary comic-book writer and magickal practitioner Grant Morrison puts it: "Magick provides a powerful context and support system for even the darkest or most fucked-up times and experiences." More than that: "magic encourages you to take charge of your own life; it confers a sense of agency and self-control that can seem lacking at times when epic, elemental forces seem to have us at their mercy."[3]

In the past few years especially, there's been a wealth of brilliant writing and resources exploring the intersections of queerness and magic. Much of this work draws parallels between the liminality and fluidity of queer sexualities, identities and experiences, and how witchcraft and magic often explore or experiment with liminal spaces and states. For some, including artist and creator of *Queer Heresies* magazine, Kevin Talmer Whiteneir Jr, this can be a potent source of power:

> Like witchcraft, sexual queerness is considered dangerous in that it disrupts familiar and accepted behaviours and boundaries of gender and sexuality. Because of this shared history, many have sought to reclaim the witch for its queer potential. Much like witches, queerness exists in a liminal space, one which blurs accepted social boundaries and is considered by social gatekeepers as a threat to religious and civil order. Witchcraft and queerness both represent forbidden knowledge and power in practice. This knowledge and power can mobilize marginalized peoples to disestablish restrictive cultural systems and, in their place, manifest realities that extend the borders of prevailing hegemonic ideas.[4]

Writing in the anthology *Arcane Perfection*, a fantastic collection of writing by queer, trans and intersex witches, G G Irkalla describes magick as being irrevocably intertwined with its political and cultural context.

> Magick, art and politics are inseparable: do not trust anyone who says otherwise. ... Queer activism fights [oppression and

---

3   "Magic Works: An Interview with Grant Morrison", *Mondo 2000*, February 2017, www.mondo2000.com/2017/08/14/magic-works-an-interview-with-grant-morrision/
4   https://activisthistory.com/2019/05/24/queer-heresies-witchcraft-and-magic-as-sites-of-queer-radicality/

exploitation] on a secular level. Queer witchcraft fights this on the spiritual level.[5]

Based on my own lived experience, work as a mental health practitioner and research and interviews for this essay, it's clear that those with marginalized identities – be it via sexuality, gender, race, class, disability, other aspects or combinations of these – face the biggest (personal, familial, systemic and institutional) barriers to fully claiming, developing and exercising their personal agency and power. In these instances, witchcraft can provide a much-needed power source, framework and language for resistance and activism.

" *... witchcraft can provide a much-needed power source, framework and language for resistance and activism.*"

Samantha Mant, a bisexual, disabled, working-class witch and naturopath, explains, "Every time I see a marginalized group practice witchcraft, there is inherent justice in that. Especially indigenous people in colonized lands. As well as the beauty and connection of the practice itself, it's a act of defiance, freedom and rebellion." Alongside specific protection spells and rituals, witchcraft as a practice and belief system can in and of itself have a fortifying and protective function. Iman of QM4R (Queer Magic for the Resistance) collective describes this:

> To me, magic IS resistance. I turned to these traditions most open-heartedly in the midst of Black Lives Matter protests c. 2014, when I started to feel hopeless and emotionally drained after regular violent confrontations with the police at demonstrations. By wielding these protective amulets, reciting these incantations, calling upon the Orishas, and working

---

5   G G Irkalla, "Men are from Earth, Women are from Earth: A Practical Guide to Gender Being Obsolete", featured in *Arcane Perfection,* Cutlines Press, 2017

intimately with the plants, stones, roots, and bones of my environment, I began to feel more empowered. Quickly my focus in the Craft moved away from damning hexes against white supremacy, to community care work and deep psycho-social-spiritual healing for black and brown people in the struggle.[6]

So where does class fit into all this? While I'm beyond grateful for the diverse range of writing on queerness and witchcraft that's become available in recent years, how these intersect with class, poverty and their impact on the accessibility of witchcraft remains an area I'd love to see more people exploring. Like almost every witch of my generation, the 90s cult classic *The Craft* was a game-changer for me in many ways. Not least because the teen witches in it got their supplies by shoplifting (something I was also skilled and experienced at) and because Nancy – charismatic, confident Nancy, who led the coven, terrified teen boys in the school corridors and wore iconic outfits while doing it – was the poorest of the four. And through witchcraft, she changes her circumstances: in a confrontation with Nancy, her abusive stepdad has a fatal heart attack, allowing Nancy and her mother to cash out his life insurance policy, moving out of their former trailer park home to live it up in financial comfort and security for the first time in their lives.

Now, I'm not excusing *The Craft*'s problematic elements, which go way beyond the scope of this essay (Rachel True, herself a practising witch, has spoken out numerous times about how the racist abuse her character Rochelle endures in the film paralleled the racism she experienced during and post-production, and neither am I thrilled that Nancy, as the only character explicitly coming from poverty, has a narrative arc about being too power-hungry that ends with her in a psych ward). For the record, I'm also not advocating for shoplifting from your local indie metaphysical shop, should you be lucky enough to have one.

---

6   "Queer Activists Are Using Magic As Resistance", *Wear Your Voice Magazine*, 2017, https://web.archive.org/web/20210509042738/www.wearyourvoicemag.com/interview-queer-magic-resistance/

But watching those scenes so many decades ago still resonates with me now, in part of because its answer to the questions I had then: How do you learn about this? Where do you get the books? The materials? And what if you can't afford it?

Existing as we do under capitalism, there's an ongoing tension between accessibility and ensuring people are fairly paid for their time, labour, goods and services. And it's a tension that's impacted the practice of the queer working-class witches I spoke to for this essay. As Samantha Mant explains:

> As a teen and younger woman, I couldn't always afford the 'required' ingredients for a ritual or spell. This led to me using visualization more in my work, or learning to substitute with herbs etc. more in sync with my local area, or being creative on my own terms. I also became mindful of the magic and resources of the land I live on, and what it meant to be respectful as a white woman on colonized land.

Creativity catalysed by scarcity was a response echoed in Grant Morrison's approach:

> Instead of a traditional wand, I had a little wand from a magic set my parents gave me when I was a kid, just one of those little black and white conjuror ones. The dagger was one a friend had brought me from Istanbul; the Lamp an old railway man's lamp found at the side of the tracks. I made my own tarot pack with Polaroid pictures of places and things that were meaningful to me – the Key, the Fountain, the Bridge. It was all about this kind of homemade, DIY. Chaos punk magic. I had this kitchen-sink shaman approach and I liked translating magical practice into the everyday and ordinary. That's how I developed my own system with things that meant something personal to me as well as working with more traditional gods or ideas.[7]

---

7 "Magic Works: An Interview with Grant Morrison", *Mondo 2000*, February 2017, www.mondo2000.com/2017/08/14/magic-works-an-interview-with-grant-morrision/

Necessity has long been recognized as the mother of invention, and there's an argument that developing your own path and practice from not having access to the "proper" tools and materials might give it even more potency; perhaps that highly individualized development process creates a deeper, more personal and authentic relationship between the practitioner and their practice. But it could also lead to intimidation, a paralysis through fear of getting it "wrong", and/or a sense of exclusion from the community. Having always been told my aptitude for learning was my ticket out of poverty, I can recognize how my working-class background coupled with my longtime fascination with witchcraft led me toward extensive reading and research. I soaked up information like a sponge, but it was ages before I gave myself permission to put what I'd learned into practice. Reflecting on this, I can acknowledge the impact of my class conditioning; an internalized cultural bias about not being clever enough, or academic enough, an anxiety about having learned enough to practise ethically and responsibly. Not always being able to afford access to the "right" resources, from materials to tickets to classes and conventions, had led me – subtly, so subtly it took me a long time to recognize it – to a subconscious fear of being somehow "found out" and shamed if anyone realized my personal framework was my own homemade, DIY version of the "kitchen sink" approach Grant Morrison describes.

For others, though, there's a freedom and playfulness in coming to witchcraft on their terms. For all its challenges, that's the fierce defiance and joy of outsider status, a role the queer working-class witches in my community proudly embrace. Anne Louise Kershaw, who creates art under the moniker Synda Sova, describes this further:

I haven't come at anything in my life from a 'learn-ed' place, a place of knowing the 'right' way of doing a thing, from books or heritage or ancestries. I've come at it raw, with enthusiasm and passion and joy to find my way through it. Because of this, I don't get het up on the actuality of ritual,

*definitions, moon cycles, meanings of things as they've been
categorized by others. I make it up as I go along. And make
it up again anew whenever I like. When you aren't told there's
a way to do things you're also not told there's a way not to.*

Inventiveness, fluidity and agility of response to context and need
were also recognized as important in G G Irkalla's writing; their
list of "important elements to queer witchcraft" included "being
dirty, glitter, individuality, body modification, giving each other
tattoos, helping each other emotionally prepare for surgeries
or to recover after." Following on from this, their summary of
tools and weapons of queer witchcraft included brass knuckles,
broken mirrors, binders and glitter bombs[8] (a list that served as
inspiration for the title of this essay). All of which speak to the role
of resourcefulness and creativity in the face of adversity, and how
for people facing marginalization across class, sexuality or other
identity factors, this ability to adapt and incorporate available
resources can support both the practice itself and a more general
sense of resilience, strength or protection for the practitioners.
This is especially true for someone with history of experiencing
violence – for example, being armoured with tools that if
necessary could serve as both practical and magickal weapons
might provide a sense of safety and security. Like many women,
queer and trans people, I have the habit of walking home at night
with my keys held like blades between my knuckles. I own several
spiked rings whose specific purpose is making me feel safer; should
I ever be attacked, and be able to retaliate, I know they'd do some
damage, hopefully causing my assailant to retreat or be marked
for future identification. Making a ritual of putting on these rings
with the intention that they'll protect me makes me more able to
navigate certain environments, reducing my fear and anxiety.

I could write an entire other essay about witchcraft and its
potential applications in trauma recovery, and all the working-

---

8   G G Irkalla, "The Lament of Agdistis", featured in *Arcane Perfection,* Cutlines
Press, 2017

class queer witches I talked to for this piece had a lot to say about the therapeutic benefits of their magickal practice. Again, the protective, strengthening function of witchcraft emerged as a key theme, and one which makes sense as something having massive value for a people with histories of marginalization and oppression. Samantha Mant described her process of using visualisation for protection:

> I see flames around myself or loved one, protecting them, or a sword hanging in the air in front of their heart. I've called on the archetypal goddess energy of The Morrigan in ritual to protect family or friends in dire need. Every time I've used witchcraft for protection has made me feel a fierce sense of empowerment and calm. A reassurance that all will be well, that the universe has it own definition and terms for justice.

This was echoed by artist, writer and activist Ally Davies:

> I'm a worrier, always have been. I worry about violence, injury, accidents, bad health, disasters and crime. I regularly use crystals, do spells and rituals, make protective moon water, sigils and charge protective talismans like sea stones, crystals, sea shells and coral to use in our house, car, on myself and the beings closest to me. I use them all the time and hope and believe they protect us from harm.

Samantha Mant also recognized the role of witchcraft in discharging her anger about injustice, and responding with self-compassion:

> Embodying my anger helps my nervous system process and release it. I turn it into a ritual. I listen for the clarity it gives me on actions to take. Anger is a great motivator and informs where we may need to fortify or create stronger boundaries. I can also use anger to petition spirit for protection, for myself or others.

But by far and away the most significant takeaway from my conversations was how central a role witchcraft and magick has in cultivating self-acceptance. "My practice has brought me self-confidence, reliance, resilience, empowerment, healing, education, compassion and understanding for the plight of others," Samantha Mant explains. "Witchcraft is my healing work, my self-care, my activism, my learning."

"Witchcraft and magick mean everything to me," Ally Davies reflected. "To me, it's like coming home. Practising as a witch has helped my depression and helped me discover peace and happiness, and who I am. Tapping into this power, I love feeling equal to nature and feeling like we stand together: if I fall back, I am caught by this beautiful parent that is always there and has always been there through all of time. It means the world to me."

Building on this further, Ally described a significant shift in self-acceptance relating to their sexuality and genderfluidity: "Witchcraft makes me feel I can be anything. For me, witchcraft is all about deep communion with nature, and my gender, sexuality and queerness are so natural they feel synonymous with magick." Ally also experienced other transformational change since exploring witchcraft:

What have I gained? Self trust definitely. Self assurance. Inner peace, hope, connection to a community of other people like me. Connection to my creativity I thought I'd lost. Connection to a bigger world. Connection to nature. Seeing the love in the dark and the light. Connection to positivity, hope and happiness – I struggled so long with severe depression, suicidal ideation and low self-worth. But witchcraft has brought me things I never had before. I never thought I could be a positive person or someone with hope. It's given me more compassion and the ability to connect with others more. It's brought me new, amazing relationships with people, friends and my coven. It's given me more purpose and direction in other parts of my life. It's made me want to connect more with everything and be a better person.

From a personal perspective, I've had parallel experiences; my self-trust, courage and sense of connection to nature, magick and community have all increased exponentially as I've explored and developed my own witchcraft path and practice. But maybe more importantly, the consensus from my reading, research and interviews was a theme of witchcraft representing a return of some kind, perhaps to a state prior to experiencing the challenges, barriers and sometimes trauma that queerness and poverty can entail. Not necessarily to wholeness, but a sense of perspective, integration and healing. Anne Louise Kershaw explained it like this:

> *Witchcraft has given me a return to myself. I always had it, magic: a connection with myself and nature, naivety, innocence, creativity, imagination, instinct, something inside of me that is far more ancient in terms of ancestral memory and connectivity to the universal. Then it all got lost, religioned, maladapted, hurt and abandoned. And magic, that line within myself that has remained true and real and connected, has enabled me to find my way back to it all. Now I feel at once young and old. Innocent and wise. A seedling and ancient. Full circle, solid and liquid, simultaneously standing still and flowing.*

Whether it's through dirt or glitter, visualization, ritual, making seashell talismans or smashing mirrors, these states of connection, self-acceptance, plurality and empowerment are things I hope all my queer working-class siblings find in their own witchcraft practice.

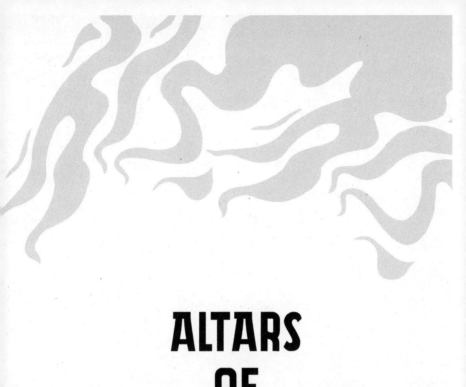

ALTARS
OF
TRANSITION

"*Around the altar's edge are five elemental talismans, each gifted ...*"

3

ALTARS OF TRANSITION

BY HARRY JOSEPHINE GILES

Content note: *includes description of ritual genital body modification and state medical violence.*

*B*y my desk is an eight-sided, dark-stained wooden altar. It's still as battered as when I found it, under a heap of furniture in a second-hand shop on Easter Road, the last post-gentrification holdout of Leith's house-clearing trade. Around the altar's edge are five elemental talismans, each gifted: a blue patch embroidered with ice creams and red flames, sent by a good old friend in the post; a butterfly wing, found by a good new friend on a walk in the island of Hoy, Orkney, and carried safely home; a black patch with a pink triangle, offered by a favourite bookshop for strength in a heavy time; a hare's leg-bone, stripped clean and presented by the sun at Hermaness, Shetland, in sight of the Muckle Flugga light; and a grey sea pebble, found by a stranger and delivered by another, the three of us connected by tenuous social media presences, because strange time saw fit to carve it with four clean lines, three straight and one curved, marking out the initials of my chosen name.

In the centre of my altar, charged by these items and buttressed by the tarot cards I draw each day, are two medications: a glass vial of estradiol valerate wrapped in tin foil, and an orange cardboard packet of progesterone labelled in cyrillic text. I paid for both through online money transfer services, one via an email address texted to me in an encrypted chat, one via a grey pharmacy website that's since been shut down. Twice a week my boifriend injects me from the vial, in a functional little ritual involving plastic gloves and alcohol swabs; each evening I take the squishy ball of progesterone inside myself.

The altar is often dusty and some mornings I neglect to refresh the cards. Some nights I fall into bed forgetting the pill; some days I fret at my crashing energy until I realize that my body is crying out for the estrogen I should have injected hours ago. I am not a consistent witch, and my structures of routine often fail. But still, through the application of this magic my body has changed, growing lines and curves where none were before, advancing and retreating in expected and unexpected ways. One day these spells and their habits might bring an equilibrium, but for now all is change. I ask the altar, the vial, the pills, the cards and the talismans to hold me steady as the world shifts around my shifting self.

~~ ~~ ~~ ~~ ~~

In a corner of the British Museum are two serrated bronze bars, little-known and rarely noticed. The bars each end in a hinged hoop, and are decorated with the heads of animals and deities. They were found in the Thames in 1840, and are dated to second- or third-century Roman culture. Along the flanks are the gods of the planets and the days. Saturn, Apollo, Diana, Mars, Mercury, Jupiter and Venus are recognisable from their marks; the eighth is now worn away, but carries what looks like an agricultural crown, for Ceres and the eighth market day. Above and below are stallions and bulls and on top, facing out toward the congregation, are Cybele and Attis.

The memory of Cybele, a mother goddess, is often suppressed, but for a few millennia either side of the birth of Christ she and her consort Attis were worshipped. The tradition began in the lands east of the Mediterranean and was semi-integrated into classical Greek and Roman cultures, from there extending through the Roman empire as far as Londinium, where this tool was used. Roman historians describe the faith's ecstatic rituals and its priests, the *galli*, who wore bright clothes, heavy jewellery and make-up, who bleached and crimped their hair, and who were castrated. The bars in the British Museum are castration clamps, used in the Londonium temple to initiate *galli*. At some point the clamps were deliberately broken and cast into the river. The historian Alfred Francis speculated about a third century raid into the Temple of the Magna Mater: devotees of Christ fighting to end the worship of Cybele and its transgender rituals.[1]

In some tellings Cybele was the mother of Attis, in others Attis's lover, in others both. In some tellings Cybele was also the mother of the dual-sexed Agditis whose penis and testicles were cut off by displeased gods, the organs then growing a tree that fed a nymph who gave birth to Attis; in other versions Cybele was herself Agditis; and in all tellings when Agditis or Cybele or both appeared in her full glory to Attis, Attis went mad, self-castrated, died, was resurrected and became eternally devoted to the goddess. This story is the origin of the ancient Rome's Day of Blood on March 24th, when after days of mourning and abstinence the novitiate priests of Cybele flogged and castrated themselves in an orgiastic ceremony, throwing blood and body parts onto Cybele's altar. The next sunrise marked the Day of Joy and Relaxation – may we all have such days.

In the classical sources the *galli* are named sometimes as he, sometimes as she, and sometimes as a third sex. They are always feminized and frequently racialized – their skin, clothing and music marking the tradition's origins east of the empire. This religion, and in particular its castration rituals, was at times tolerated by the Roman state and at times rendered taboo. Castration, embraced by the *galli*, was feared by power for its potential. For extended periods, Rome itself

---

1 Francis, AG, "On a Romano-British Castration Clamp used in the Rights of Cybele", *Proceedings of the Royal Society of Medicine*, 1926, 19 (Sect Hist Med), 95-110

appointed an *archigallus* to oversee the faith, and some have argued that this overseer was never themself castrated: a citizen manager of Cybele's unruly transgender spirituality, a means of restraining mother-worship's cuts across Roman authority.

The *Greek Anthology* records this prayer, naming Cybele as Rhea and her worshipper as a castrated he: "The long-haired priest of Rhea, the newly gelded, the dancer from Lydian Tmolus whose shriek is heard afar, dedicates, now he rests from his frenzy, to the solemn Mother who dwells by the banks of Sangarius these tambourines, his scourge armed with bones, these noisy brazen cymbals, and a scented lock of his hair."[2]

~~~ ~~~ ~~~ ~~~

My hormonal metamorphosis, my transition, began with two rituals. The first ritual involved paying a private doctor, completing a lengthy questionnaire about my sex and gender history, sitting through a video consultation and receiving a psychiatric diagnosis of gender dysphoria. This is the State's ritual of transition, here greased by private savings to slip by the NHS's intolerable waiting times. This initiation led, after a fistful of months, to a prescription, and then an order, and then a delivery.

The second ritual was a ceremony with seven of my closest friends. I devised it myself, based on my rough self-tutelage in practical magic. We placed ourselves in a circle, seven flesh bodies and one digital, attending by laptop. I opened the circle with words and cards, protected it with salt, lit a candle. We each wrote on slips what it was about our genders that we wanted to let go, placed the papers in a central bowl and burned them. We each wrote what it was about our genders that we wanted to welcome and invited these words into our bodies, anointed with a drop of water charged under the full moon. Finally, my loving boifriend opened the foil packet of

2   Paton WR, *Greek Anthology*, Book VI, 237, p.427, Heinemann, 1926

an Evorel® 50μg estradiol patch and applied it to my hip. We sat quietly and then I thanked everyone, thanked the spirits, blew out the candle and opened the circle. There were cheers.

Each of these rituals was made possible by the other. Too afraid of my desire, and too afraid of the consequences of sourcing my own hormones through barely legitimate means, I sought the approval of a doctor whom I paid for the service and the security of a traceable pharmaceutical supply chain, which I also paid for. Without those authorities, I don't know if I could have brought myself into ritual. But without the solidarity of my temporary coven and the necessary magic of my devised ceremony, I don't know if I could have lived with the powers I had brought into my life. The collective consecration of my transition began a teasing apart of juridical medicine that has only unravelled further since.

I had thought that I was inviting the magic into my body to assist the hormones in doing their work. In a sense this was what happened but, as is usually the case with magic, it happened counter to all expectation. The specific arrangement of carbon, hydrogen and oxygen could theoretically have begun doing its work without any spell at all – at least, I've heard of plenty of women who've managed without the magic. Estradiol rearranges flesh and synapse quite happily and suppresses testosterone, only one carbon atom and four hydrogen atoms apart, in good time. But as the gift settled into me, became part of me, it transformed my attitude to power itself.

The short story: by the time the NHS's psychiatry-dominated Gender Identity Clinic finally saw me, seven years after I had begun to summon myself through names, clothes, allies and ritual motions, three years after I was referred by a GP, two years after I started taking hormones, I no longer had faith in or need for medical approval. At that point, I was buying hormones on the internet, and GIC doctors were rarely able to provide me with the support and oversight I needed. Instead, I turned to Reddits and Discords and Signal chats, to collective knowledge and experimentation, to my sisters.

The Spring 1994 issue of *TransSisters*, the short-lived Journal of Transsexual Feminism that emerged from North American trans women's political movements, contains retellings of the Cybele myth and history, and also a condensed liturgy for the rites of Cybele and Attis.[3] There is an account of the ceremony's performance, and many involved in the journal and the ritual are names familiar to the history of 90s transfeminism. *TransSisters* was a key player in the conflicts around Michigan Womyn's Music Festival, beginning with the exclusion in 1991 of trans woman Nancy Jean Burkholder, and leading to the establishment of Camp Trans, which fomented much of the radical thought that shapes trans liberation movements today.

TransSisters closed in acrimony in the mid-90s, broken by burnout and internal fights, and by the strains of the MichFest conflict. The struggle spectacularized the trans-exclusionary tendency within feminism now taking the world stage, and also shaped opposing camps within the trans community that still persist, such as a putative opposition between trans women who undergo genital surgery and trans women who do not. The revived Maetrum of Cybele, however, continues, operating physically out of the Catskill Mountains and digitially at gallae.com. The new *galli* officiate weddings and memorials, and their temple has operated as shelter for homeless trans people.

This is one telling of transfeminist history and trans women's spirituality in one contemporary settler-colonial site. It is a white-dominated telling, shaped also by the class positions of those involved. This was noted at the time: *TransSisters*' riotous zine contemporary, *Gendertrash*, published in Toronto, ran

3 Gabriel DA and Skyclad Publishing Co., *TransSisters: The Journal of Transsexual Feminism,* No.4, Spring 1994, Digital Transgender Archive, www.digitaltransgenderarchive.net/files/79407x266

a 1995 article from Christine Tayleur lambasting the white middle-class tendency. "While a few people run off and spend a $1000 to lounge around in hot-tubs or to protest transsexual exclusion at the MWMF, the majority of our population is excluded from basic human rights,"[4] she wrote, going on to highlight struggles against incarceration, psychiatrization, violence, homelessness, racism, poverty and AIDS.

Similarly, the incorporation of Greco-Roman history into the white supremacist narratives of European empire shapes the Cybele revival's all-too-common whiteness. The revival's resistance to patriarchy, Christianity and imperial faith is constructed by the whiteness of what it resists, bound up with whiteness's constructed claim on north Mediterranean antiquity. The twentieth century fascist salute is a reconstruction of the French Revolutionary painter David's eighteenth century reconstruction of a seventh century BCE Roman salute; such layers of storytelling obscure the racial complexities and diversities of classical north Mediterranean cultures, and also the racialization of the *galli* themselves within the Roman empire. My own interest in the *galli* is not independent of these troubling affinities and heritages.

Broader histories of trans spirituality have always been told. Another writer would consider the eighteenth century black Haitian revolutionary leader Romaine-la-Prophetesse, whose blending of Catholic and Vodou practices reached back to the feminized religious figures of West Central Africa,[5] or Sylvia Rivera's use of holy altars and spiritual weaponry in the twentieth century STAR House for mostly Latino street queens.[6]

Just as there is no universal spirituality, there is no universal transition: transness is shaped by race, class, geography,

---

4 Tayleur C, "Racism and Poverty in the Transgender Community", in MacKay XP and Ross M-S, *Gendertrash From Hell,* No.4, Spring, 1995, Digital Transgender Archive, www.digitaltransgenderarchive.net/files/02870w08h
5 Rey, Terry, *The Priest and the Prophetess,* Oxford University Press, 2017
6 *Street Transvestite Action Revolutionaries: survival, revolt, and queer antagonist struggle,* Untorelli Press, 2013

history and all the dynamics of power. Complex stories cannot be recruited for simple stories of transness and magic. We can ask, though, why reaching for the spiritual dimensions of transition, or transition through spirituality, is such a common feature of trans lives and trans cultures, and why twisted threads of spirituality, mutual aid and revolution run through diverse transfeminist cultures. Morgan M Page, a trans historian who has documented many of these stories on her podcast *One From the Vaults*, suggests that trans revolutionaries' resistance to the State and State medicine is part of what leads us to spirituality. "If we depathologize transness," she says, "and we demedicalize it [...] the only explanation we are left with is the spiritual."[7]

My own ritual, conducted around the wintery northern dark of Samhain's purifying fires, was also a ritual castration. I use the word in full knowledge of its violence, and in knowledge that, like all the technologies of transition, what castration contains is more complex and delightful than what the phallocentric cisgender world imagines. The *galli*'s castration may have involved penectomy, orchidectomy, vasectomy, circumcision, any combination of the four, or other changes we've failed to imagine. Contemporary transfeminine genital surgery can involve some of these, and also penile inversion vaginoplasty, zero depth vaginoplasty, scrotal labioplasty, and/or erectile tissue clitoroplasty: technologies of embodiment and sexual fulfilment. It is hard now to know what any individual Roman *gallus* wanted, or what "wanted" means in their terms, but surely most pursued such changes through their willed ecstasy, their madness.

My madness was not induced by a Roman street sex party but sought in a psychiatric Skype call; it was not an altered

---

7   Page, MM, "OFTV Presents - Interview with Abram J Lewis", Podcast, 2021, https://soundcloud.com/onefromthevaultspodcast/oftv-presents-interview-with-abram-j-lewis (Accessed Jan 26 2022)

mental state but a medical diagnosis. Still, madness was a gateway to further body modification, new drugs I could not otherwise afford and brief glimmers of medical support. One drug I now use, estrogen, was also used to chemically castrate Alan Turing, giving him the gender dysphoria it treats in me; another, triptorelin, has been used to chemically castrate perpetrators of sexual violence. These drugs are also used to treat endometriosis and prostate cancer, and for birth control. Their effect on me is a serious shift in sexual desire, function and behaviour: an end to the phallus and the beginning of an exploration of the ways my body makes meaning.

"If transition is subject to medical supervision, then my spells have surprises in store for my doctors"

This entangling of the technologies of punishment, treatment and self-fulfilment is not unique to transition but is common to all spiritual practices. In one body and social regime, a technology suppresses unwanted behaviours; in another body and its counter-culture, the same technology opens up new pleasures and ways of knowing. Phallocentric culture assumes that castration is about destroying masculinity and its power; for me, emasculation does not register as a meaningful term in the face of the transformation I have pursued, and my power now is truer and greater.

But the authorized spaces of transition are still pathologically unmagical. The state and capital make of gender, that infinite space of play and violence, an exercise in administration, a will-to-boredom that crushes transition's unruly desires with a force as powerful as it is disguised. The human in transition identifies a blasphemous need, and on presenting this need to the forces of order is given waiting lists, hold music, dropdown gender menus, deed polls, before and after photos, forms in triplicate, snake oil inclusion, bleached paper, awkward pauses, autoresponders, answering machines, invoices, email surveys, pronoun signatures, media requests, lowered gazes, gates, unexplained delays, checking with the supervisor, exasperated refusals, call transfers, fugitive letters, bursting fileboxes, bitterness, envy, papercuts, sticky tape, staplers, enemies, and all the other accessories of the management of life. The grand scale of sexed bureaucracy is itself a reminder of the perversity of the trans request.

Magic, then, is a muddy track running underneath the powerlines. If transition is subject to medical supervision, then my spells have surprises in store for my doctors. If transition is afforded some small space by government, then my covens dance circles around my administrators. And if transition rings the till for petty merchants, then I call on my guiding spirits to overturn the exchange. My self-castration was negotiated with state medicine, and its growing potential has brought me into the spiritual community of transfeminism, rebelling against the powers through which it happened.

Like Page, I do want to describe transition as a spiritual calling, but I also struggle under such a weight. I do not want to have to be a priest in order to exist, perceived only in mythic terms – a cisheteropatriarchal lens on transness that does less to liberate and more to constrain. Transition happens to material flesh in messy reality. I did, however, need a spiritual practice in order to transition, and call on the power of magic to do what is necessary for my body, self and story. Transition is an act forbidden by order, but magic disorders possibility. Transition is still so much an impossible and unknowable thing, but magic is doing without knowing, becoming without being, the spiritual practice of hope.

After my hormone ritual, I was supposed to bury the ashes in a safe and distant place, keeping the participants safe from their relinquished genders. I did not. Instead, I placed the ashes in an

IKEA sandwich bag, and the bag in a drawer I rarely open, and forgot about them. Two years after I began hormone therapy, when the NHS Gender Identity Clinic finally opened its doors to me, I opened that drawer and the bag of ashes fell into my hand.

I felt a terrible and typical shame; I had done the magic poorly, and so done harm to our lives. Had I trapped my coven in an unfinished ritual, and what constraints had that placed around their gendered selves? But the full moon was approaching with my psychiatric appointment, and I found the necessary strength. I lit a candle and drew three tarot cards for past, present and future: the Knight of Wands, the Chariot and the Ten of Cups. (I leave the interpretation to you, offering two guides: Pamela Colman Smith, the queer artist whose 1909 designs for the so-called Rider-Waite tarot, particularly her new minor arcana, defined the first tarot revival; and Rachel Pollack, the science-fiction author, contributor to *TransSisters* and co-founder of the London Gay Liberation Front's trans wing, whose 1980 book *78 Degrees of Wisdom* defined the second.) After the reading, I cycled to a bridge, crossing the point where my home's river, the Water of Leith, meets the sea. A crèche of eiders was watching. I spoke the words of release. I emptied the ashes into the water. The wind tugged at me, and the first few drops of rain fell.

> "... magic is doing without knowing, becoming without being, the spiritual practice of hope."

Magic, like transition, has risks, and it can go wrong. I have continued to adjust and question my own medication regimes, struggling as changes happened too slowly, or too quickly, desired and undesired. The more powerful and meaningful the ritual, the greater the care and attention it requires. It will always be easy to do unintended harm. Neither magic nor transition can or should be ceded to authority, least of all the

authority of the sovereign self. Magic and transition belong
to history and community, are negotiations between a person
and the world. I devise my own rituals and I manage my
own transition, but I do neither alone. I study grimoires and
hormone tables, I consult with elders and doctors, and I am
in continual communication with my coven, my sisters. Not
Do-It-Yourself, but Do-It-Together. The first easy secret of
transition is that it can be broken free from power: you can just
find hormones and take them. The second harder secret is that
doing so well takes much more care and responsibility than
giving power over to authority, which is why it's worth doing.

Still, my magic is as shabby as my transition. I eye the
practices of better witches as I do the transitions of beautiful
women, imagining that they would never stammer a spell,
drop their tuck, let their herbs rot, be unable to admit the truth
to their parents, forget the moon, delay their appointments,
wait so long, wait so long. Envy is poison to magic and far
less real. Every witch has a failed spell and I do not know a
woman who has not wished her transition otherwise. This
is to say that I work to be careful, and when I am careless I
work for forgiveness. Equally, as much as I wish all hormones
into anarchy and chafe against the ignorant authority of
bad doctors, there are times I am glad of the support of a
knowledgeable and kind practitioner within a public health
service, and times when the conventional opinions of a DIY
community are as constraining as any psychiatrist's. My
magical transition is syncretic: I take what I need from the
systems of power and unpower I live in, and work to give
back threefold. When a sister asks how to work a spell I have
worked, I share with her what I can and what I can't; when
a sibling needs support to develop their own magic, I will
give what lore and equipment I have. Transition is an unruly
coven, and its altar carries us all.

"Envy is poison to magic and far less real."

MENTAL HEALTH AND MAGIC

"When I think of the magic moving through my body, I often think of my late Sicilian grandmother..."

4

MENTAL HEALTH & MAGIC: ON FORGING A PATH THROUGH THE DARKNESS, TOGETHER

BY LISA MARIE BASILE

*W*hen I think of the magic moving through my body, I often think of my late Sicilian grandmother, Concetta (who, in America, called herself Mary), for she indirectly influenced it.

She was born in Palermo in 1921. I can see her through invented, sepia-toned memories, hanging her linen laundry on a line in the sun or seeking shade under the generous lemon trees during a time when many southern Italian and Sicilian families deeply struggled.

In real life, I remember her mumbling in dialect before her home altars and shrines, or scribbling little prayers and notes of request, which she'd place before tiny statuettes of the saints.

I can remember being sent bottles of energy-cleansing holy water in the mail, and mentions of *il mal'occhio*, the evil eye's unlucky condition, which could be alchemized and removed with sacred words, olive oil and salt. (Have you ever felt a sudden haze of malaise, headache or inexplicable sorrow? According to folk tradition, you may have been struck by an intentional or rogue evil eye).

These traditions – however influenced by organized religion or folk practices or Paganism, and all the inevitable intersections therein – swim around us in our mundane lives, born from some primal wellspring found in every culture. These traditions tell us we all house an inherent ability to heal; and so we gaze into history to move forward through our lives.

To some, these acts have no formal name. Some might call it folk magic. Some might call it shamanism. Some might even call it a placebo effect. And some might call it witchcraft. Whatever it is, these age-old practices – which ultimately hinge on a belief in some potent, mysterious, invisible force – help us to find autonomy and comfort. Healing magic is bone, blood and root – waiting to be tapped into, and as natural as breathing.

My grandmother turned to these practices in times of pain and crisis – and although "mental health" was not a subject she would have spoken of, magical or magically-influenced practices do offer ways to help manage our anxiety, depression and even PTSD.

REWRITING THE NARRATIVE

Magic is a way of setting the tides in motion and even righting the scoreboard, but it is also a tool for holistic personal wellness. For example, casting a spell calls on our presentness – our tuning in. It requires us to recite the poetry of the liminal (what exists in the lightless cracks?) and recognize the exquisite connection between all things. How does trauma affect our mental state, and how does that affect how we treat others? And how does that trickle down into everything else?

And just like my grandmother – who, over a fragrant vat of *pasta con le sarde*, might mumble a few key words to keep her children happy and healthy, or who kept candles lit for the saints of joy and hope – contemporary witches use magic to ask these important questions and hopefully find some answers (and relief).

When I started writing my first nonfiction book, *Light Magic for Dark Times: Spells, Rituals and Practices for Coping in a Crisis*, it was abundantly clear to me that magic was shimmering through the collective consciousness.

More and more craft books were being published and more conversations were being had, especially by people who hadn't come from a lineage of magic or who were new to magic. Fireflies were fluttering through the darkness. Suddenly, friends who weren't exactly spiritual were sharing their dreams and asking questions about synchronicities. We'd have adult slumber parties, up all night casting little spells and pulling oracle cards and talking about invisible pathways of magic.

An ember of hope has been struck into a flame, I texted a friend after we did a grief ritual (which ended up in my book). *My sadness has become more bearable*, they wrote back. It's palpable. They said they went home and built an altar dedicated to all the things that brought them joy and purpose. Our ritual had allowed us to grieve, to make space for joy, to give pain meaning.

It dawned on me that we did this because there were no immediate community resources at our disposal for grief management. Therapists can be too expensive. Religion didn't offer the answers we needed. And society turns away from overt gestures of grief. Witchcraft gave us the permission to build our own space for sorrow. Ritual gave us the structure. A spell, in the form of a poem, gave us the language. This was personal and communal self-care.

This rediscovery of magic (for better or worse) is cyclical and absolutely nothing new, but in 2017 when I was writing my book it was especially potent. The social and political landscape in the US and elsewhere was (and is) ravaged by racism, sexism, anti-LGBTQIA rhetoric, acts of aggression against indigenus people and the land and self-interested politicians.

People were (and are) exhausted by patriarchal, oppressive institutions and dangerous, brewing political ideologies – and many seek a way to clear their energy and find hope in small, sacred moments. In some sense, magic offers people – especially those most oppressed – a way to decolonize the self.

"The challenge of today's witch is to fully embrace our bodies and tap into our personal power, despite what constructs and limitations society may seek to place upon us," writes Laura

Tempest Zakroff in *Anatomy of a Witch*. "Through those lived experiences, we gain the wisdom to connect with the seen and unseen worlds, as well as each other. We become truly ourselves – capable, present, and powerful."[1]

And so, more and more people are seeking free, alternative methods of self-care. It seems as though society is still blooming, rewriting a narrative toward self- and community-care: we do not have to rely on systems that ultimately do not benefit nor heal us. We can use what time has taught us – about nature, about ritual, about the potency of the unknown – to do it ourselves.

"The challenge of today's witch is to fully embrace our bodies and tap into our personal power"

I see this in everything. People want to take care of their communities and their households in intentional and meaningful ways, and so contemporary witches create covens and digital spaces where people share healing, age-old, witchcraft remedies (like collecting St John's Wort on Midsummer Eve to ward away negativity and bad dreams or, more easily, burning the words "anxiety" or "worry" in a mini-cauldron).

People want to decompress after long working hours and commutes and nonstop protests and social media overstimulation, and so we light a candle and smoke-cleanse our homes. People want to find joy again after being flattened out by the tireless screeching of capitalism, so we embrace the sacredness of rest and wear a necklace of vervain for wellbeing.

Just swipe through social media and you'll see ingredients for stress-relieving ritual baths, tarot card prompts for self-reflection, earthing ideas for anxiety relief and more. The collective is singing, "We want to heal." It's easy to scoff at

---

1   Zakroff, Laura Tempest, Anatomy of a Witch, Llewellyn Publications, 2020

the social media witch, but the battle cry is real. We are turning to one another – and to ourselves – for a deeper reason.

We want to rewrite the narratives that have been written for and about us. We want to reclaim our identities and our bodies and the liminalities we embody.

And now, in 2021, we want to find ways to grieve and ritualistically memorialize the dead in a global pandemic. For example, at Catland Books, an occult shop and event space in Brooklyn, NY, death witch Hannah Haddadi held a masterclass on sacred grief, which offered tools such as rituals, herbal allies and flower essences to help us tend to grief. Magic is everywhere, and its connection to our psychological wellbeing is undeniable.

Bit by bit, these acts rewire the minds. According to Judith S Beck, PhD, "The way people actually get better is by making small changes in their thinking and behaviour every day."

By showing up to these practices, we are showing up to ourselves, showing up to our power – an act of self-care that can help us move through the darkest moments. If nothing else, it gives us space to take action when we are told we cannot.

For all of us, especially the marginalized – who have been told they are powerless – this is a radical rejection of that notion.

Kristen Sollée, author of the recent *Witch Hunt*, once told me, "Being so divested from nature in a capitalist, patriarchal society that relies upon self-subjugation makes nature-based practices like witchcraft a vital avenue for self-care."

AN ACCESSIBLE MAGIC IS A HEALING MAGIC

The contemporary witch is finding ways to make magic their own, to write their own spells and to create healing through accessibility and intuition.

"Finding ways to access your own intuition is the very centre of witchcraft practice, as I see it. If you're guided by your intuition, you can't really avoid magic," says Mya Spalter in *Enchantments: A Modern Witch's Guide to Self-Possession*.[2]

2   Spalter, Mya, Enchantments: A Modern Witch's Guide to Self-Possession, Pisces Books, 2018

I have held this in mind as I build my own eclectic magical practice. I aim to write my own spells, ask myself what feels right and create an accessible practice so that I can actually tend to it, rather than view it as work or a chore. Because in the tending-to is the transformation.

One night, during a blazing full moon, I planned an intuitive ritual. I found myself collecting bits and pieces from around my Brooklyn apartment, things that simply felt right. I burned rosemary to cleanse my space. I pulled my Wild Unknown deck from the shelves and created a mini altar across my mantlepiece dedicated to The Star, the card I turn to for hope and transformation in times of distress. I lit several white votive candles, which danced as sparkling stars when the night fell. I decorated with crystals to represent my needs – rose quartz for grace and love, smoky quartz to dissipate negativity.

I set a small mirror down so that I could see my own reflection, gaze into my shadow self and acknowledge its impact and influence. "Retreating into your sacred space can help you communicate with your shadow. Constructive time together lessens the deadly blow of the force she brings when a crack opens for her to creep through," writes Theresa Reed in *Tarot for Troubled Times*.[3]

I poured water into a shell as a symbol of my adaptability. I lit an incense cone to represent the blowing away of pain. I placed flowers – a dried rose, a marigold, baby's breath – throughout, simply because they are beautiful. And, like my nonna did, I wrote my desires on bay leaves, an inherited healing magic moving through me.

> *"Retreating into your sacred space can help you communicate with your shadow."*

---

3   Reed, Theresa and Shaheen Miro, Tarot for Troubled Times, Red Wheel, 2019

I made the moment mean something. I tended to my heart as a wild garden, with softness, focus and intuition. I believed that my anxiety and worry could be alleviated, at least a bit, by this ritual.

Gazing at my altar, I felt I showed up for my own mind. I looked into, rather than away from, the pain. I created a sacred space to heal, integrating both luminosity and my shadow self.

THE NEED FOR NUANCE & ACCOUNTABILITY

Witches today have a deep responsibility to ourselves and to others; we often do the heavy work of caring and acknowledging when the world does not care or see. We heal in ways that are deeper than flesh, and sometimes, of course, we can heal the flesh, too.

This is a responsibility of nuance and ethics and justice, especially with so many practices being so openly and widely shared and discussed. With so much trending around witchcraft (again, for better or for worse), it's easy to think we can turn to magic for just about anything. We cannot. And that we can turn to any form of magic whenever we want. We must not.

Some forms of magic are simply not open to us – meaning we are not entitled to the practices held sacred to certain groups. We must grapple with that entitlement and rid ourselves of appropriation. And we must learn what can and cannot be cured by magic. Ritual can empower us. It can offer reflection. It can alchemize feelings. But therapists, doctors, medication and professional medical care are also important.

We cannot bypass the very real needs of people who are mentally ill or chronically ill because we believe magic is enough, that being spiritual enough will save us, or that if our "vibes" are high, no bad will befall us.

We are natural beings; our bodies will die. Our minds will swell with sorrow. Our nervous systems will weep for protection. Our genetic predispositions will bloom, sometimes painfully. Our patience and resilience will wear thin under the crush of reality. And so we must be careful with our language when we talk about magic. It is curative, but it's not always the cure. It can hold us in its arms, but it works alongside nature, the body and the pathways of science. Magic is but one tool – and what a tool it is.

No matter the spiritual path or the personal journey, we magic-makers must work together to share resources, tell stories and encourage one another in our paths toward healing. Even the solitary practitioner must turn outward from time to time, toward the group, the coven, the world.

It is our responsibility to look into the face of the darkness and to strike a match – knowing that this will illuminate a path forward for ourselves and others.

"Magic is but one tool –
and what a tool it is."

POLITE
PERSECUTION

"I'm used to the judgement of not being considered 100 per cent 'normal'"

5

POLITE PERSECUTION:
RAISING NON–BINARY CHILDREN, DISMANTLING EVERYTHING ELSE

BY STELLA HERVEY BIRRELL

*O*t takes a village to raise a child. Everyone knows that. So off you go to your village, acquire a couple, find the other women who acquired some in the same year and make your circle around which you can raise them. Simple enough. Some might say the cackling around kitchen tables, high from homebakes and caffeine, is almost covenly. That female friendship winds bonds around your children so tight that they are always safe, always protected. That these relationships, smelted in the fire of toddlerhood and exhaustion, can never liquidate.

Unless.

What happens when your first-born starts to tell you that they aren't a girl or a boy?

What happens when one of your smelt-bonded-female-friends tells you your child has shared ideas of suicide with her child, at ten years old?

What happens when you stop? Stop trying to control the gender – even the name – of your child and realize they were never yours to control in the first place?

What happens when your village, your circle, your friend, sees you doing this, and throws you out?

What happens then?

"Now, I would like to state for the record that there were no pitchforks and no one has ever threatened to burn me."

Now, I would like to state for the record that there were no pitchforks and no one has ever threatened to burn me. In the hardship Olympics, the witches of the past win, hands down. That said, there are parallels to be drawn between parenting trans and non-binary children – affirming them – and being politely pushed into the margins where the witches live. The thing about having the first out, non-binary child in a thirty-mile radius is that there is nowhere to hide. You might as well put on a crooked black hat and grow a wart.

My oldest, from the very beginning, insisted on they/them pronouns – thankfully I no longer have to correct wait staff or people working in shops, but I did, before they started refusing to be seen in public with me at all. It's pretty easy, as evidenced by my other, binary trans child, to "pass" as any binary gender. Grow your hair, or cut it – children's bodies all look the same, (that's before you get into the whole "why are you looking at children's bodies at all?" issue). It's more difficult to ask for they/them pronouns when people are still arguing about them[1] – pronouns that felt like splintered grammar in my own mouth. Until my oldest came out, I didn't realize that adults still think of children as unfired clay, malleable figures without minds of their own. Many parents have a limited idea of who their children are, or could be. "Let kids be kids!" they say. But what they mean by that is "let kids be kids! As long as they remain binary-gendered-in-the-gender-they-were-assigned-at-birth kids!" It's less snappy that way, yes – more honest, revealing more about the space between what these people mean and what they say. Parents – adults – people on Twitter – every

---

1   www.merriam-webster.com/words-at-play/singular-nonbinary-they

major news outlet in the UK – seem to think that being gender diverse is something that parents – no, sorry, mothers, it's always mothers – do to their children. We trans them, like the witches we are! I don't understand why they think we would do this to ourselves – Munchausen's self-harm perhaps? Is that really more likely than "some children are trans"?

My belief-system had already gone three rounds with our local minister's prejudice against equal marriage, but I had taken the children to a church elsewhere. I maintain an unfashionable love and respect for ritual: lighting a candle, singing a song written two hundred years ago, giving thanks for the abundance of the harvest that now included everything I had made myself: two children and a whole heap of trouble.

TROUBLE

How can you write about micro-aggressions in a way people will understand? I'll try. A dear friend, my best mum-friend, writes an email with no transphobia in it at all, that just happened to categorize our parenting as unacceptable and our child as "the mean kid." A mum is supportive to our faces, but tells her child not to play with mine. A neighbour stops chatting, instead just waves, smiles, but crosses the road. A teacher rolls her eyes as we come into school for the third meeting that month. People at church never, ever say anything about hating the sin and loving the sinner, but there it is, on their diocesan blog. Some women have a special way of breaking those "other" women that threaten their ordered existence. They learned it from the witch-burners they are descended from.

Overt transphobia was limited to our next-door-terraced-house neighbour, with a shared driveway and a shared interest in gender identity. This women's children had played in my safe haven-house for the whole of their childhood. The payoff for my children was closed doors and closed minds.

In the end, the silence of others was as deafening as rough music, their absence as sharp as a pitchfork, but the feeling of being watched, hot as a flame.

Again, I have to admit to not being a poor thing, because we were financially able to blow up our lives and leave. I am protected by a cishet life with a cishet partner and a cishet white middle-class amount of money, unlike the witches of old. Is it really living on the margins at all, if you live on the margins but in a four-bed new build?

We took our children: one non-binary, one very recently trans, and we ran.

My mum-friend circle had dwindled, the ties that bound either cut with savage haste or quietly unwound, in the hope I wouldn't notice. One or two brave souls threw their lot in with us early on: either they were already witches, or they had actually bothered to do the reading around gender diverse children. The rest took our physical move as permission to stop answering my messages. I dream about them still, often, and wake up feeling just as hurt and broken as ever. My child uncurled inch by reversible inch, always one day forward – but a look, a word – and three days back. The trauma they had experienced was at the hands of these women's children. I had to work out what my life looked like now.

And that's when a non-mum friend started calling me a hedge witch.

BABY WITCH

Being a baby-witch is a process of taking off layers of yourself you have never questioned, never even realized were removable. It's all the easier when you have experience: removing expectations of gender being rigid and fixed was much more difficult than removing the expectation that belief-systems live in churches, mosques or temples. My experience of baby-witchhood is about returning to the earth, grounding myself, feet bare; bringing flame into daily life via my blue candle, purchased for someone who asked me to buy blue, for justice. Instead of pulling in energy through homebakes and caffeine, I find energy in solitude, in the leaves and twigs I pick up "randomly" or through a ritual found in a new book[2], and in surrounding myself with baby-witch mini-altars that I try to hide from my minimalist partner.

When people laugh at my tarot cards, I smile and agree with them. I'm used to the judgement of not being considered 100 per cent "normal" – mum-friends are generally much more interested in judgement than justice. Now I am "#blessed" by many, many people I don't know, and who have never met my child, thinking they know what's best for them,[3] so you're not going to hurt my feelings by thinking a 78-card deck can't tell the future. That's not what I use it for anyway.

So far, so introverted. You left multiple friend-circles and all you gained was a pack of cards and some gender-diverse kids? Well, yes. But I wouldn't swap it. I never considered myself a strong person until I had to fight tooth and claw for gender affirmative care for my child and a safe place for them to go to school. I never considered myself a powerful person, until I pulled the Five of Pentacles[4] for the third of three sisters in a row. As a youngest child, I've never been considered someone who could provide advice: not really. Tarot gives me the tools to talk about struggle, and hope, and help.

It's a power that used to scare me, growing up with a weird anti-witch soup: Omen films; a fear of "the devil"[5] instilled in my more fundamentalist Christian friends; a fierce belief that playing with a Ouija board could make something unidentified but terrifying happen. But the power that's within me could be harnessed by any path: religious fervour, creativity, yoga, even making a great group of friends. It's a power that's everywhere. A power made up of all the things in the universe that aren't quantifiable.

---

2   Davies, Alison, *The Mystical Year*, Quadrille, 2020, p55

3   www.gendergp.com/gender-affirmative-care-for-trans-youth/

4   For tarot meanings, I recommend www.biddytarot.com/ or Rachel Pollack's *Seventy Eight Degrees of Wisdom*

5   Whatever that means

My oldest, now a confirmed science-head, hates all this stuff, by the way. They do not like it when they pick cards, and I tell them how they feel about their own life. One week we had three different medical appointments and they drew the Ten of Wands. They didn't speak to me for the rest of the day. The next time they tried to game the tarot by asking "Is the tarot real?" and drew the Fool – the equivalent of the tarot saying "Ah, little one, you have much to learn …" They won't let me draw for them at the moment.

I found tarot after the worst of the witch hunt had passed. The people I have "lost" number in the tens, but I have gained others, some hedge-witches, some trans parents. We're disjointed, by all the broken parts we've had to put back together, and we rage for each other, clinging to those margins. We are freed from expectations, and without the noise of our insular villages or judgy mum-groups, more able to listen to our children, our selves, the earth.

> "*I found tarot after the worst of the witch hunt had passed.*"

Recently, a straggler started to disrespect my kids. As we were having it out, I kept drawing the Seven of Wands, over and over again. "Are you ready for the fight?" the tarot seemed to be asking.

"Yes, I am – look, I'm doing it right now! Jeez!"

But tarot only knows you as well as you know yourself: sometimes it's as imperfect a science as science. What it was trying to ask me was "Are you ready to give up the last circle that had held? After dismantling your belief in binary gender, your fear of witchcraft, your entire faith system, your friendship group, your home – are you now ready to dismantle your biological family?" I wasn't, and I'm still not, but here we are. I draw tarot for three of my sisters. I have four.

There are no safe havens for trans and non-binary children and their parents, just as there were no safe spaces for witches in the generations before me. The left wing is not safe, feminism isn't safe, the middle classes aren't safe. It has been an amazing, cauterizing exercise in humility and privilege to have all of these spaces – spaces that previously felt safe – removed from me. I had to find something else. And I did find something else. Halloween used to be a lovely mum-friend evening of children sweetie-eating themselves sick upstairs, while we sat and chatted over rosé and the leftover Haribo. This year, I lit candles, made tea, and drew myself The World, the Three of Pentacles (all the elements in one card), the Six of Swords (leave your shit behind you, you fool!) and the Sun. I almost believe I have all of these things.

Thanks to literally no one except their parents, my child got the care they needed, and they transformed too. Or perhaps I just "got them back." They bear the scars of trauma, but they are reawakening in ways I had forgotten to notice: wearing colours instead of black, answering questions posed by adults other than us, allowing us to hug them again.

And make no mistake about it – people still come to us, like they did to witches. When their children start questioning and their own knowledge runs out – furtively, in late-night Facebook messages, scurrying across the fields. When they come to me, I direct them to Mermaids.[6] I warn them about the fight. I light candles for them, for me, for the life I used to have, for the life I have now. For the love of the children I bore, which smelted unchanged in the white-hot fire of the most polite kind of persecution. I am broken beyond any repair (or maybe enjoying victimhood a bit too much? Ask the Ten of Swords). But in these margins, with witches of the past sending power through the veil, I know I will survive where they weren't allowed to. My children will thrive, too.

---

6   https://mermaidsuk.org.uk/

WITCH BOYS AND DEVILS ON THE ROAD

"From children's books
to political sloganeering,
our prevailing cultural
image of a witch is that of
a woman, disruptive and
out of bounds."

6

WITCH BOYS AND DEVILS ON THE ROAD: THE MAGIC OF TROUBLED MASCULINITY

BY AW EARL

"How can you know all that – you did not even see him?"

The Devil on the Road, Robert Westall [1]

From children's books to political sloganeering, our prevailing cultural image of a witch is that of a woman, disruptive and out of bounds. When we imagine a witch, her setting is rural, her social position closer to poverty than privilege and her politics at odds with the prevailing culture in which she finds herself. Yet, when asked to imagine a male magic user, the popular imagination goes to markers of education, and wealth – libraries and towers, glowing crystals and flowing robes. We might think of an alchemist surrounded by the instruments of proto-science in a secret laboratory in Prague or of John Dee summoning angels and seeking the patronage of monarchs.

---

1 Westall, Robert, *The Devil on the Road*, Penguin, 1988, p210

This is not to say that such imaginings of sorcery are without persecution, but their field is political or academic, their narrative dangers those of hubris and any violent retribution they encounter is as a result of the jealousy or ignorance of the common folk. It is an image far removed from that of a crone hunched over a bubbling cauldron or dragged from her home by the forces of the church and the law.

However, it is a matter of historical record that people once believed male witches could be found outside of institutions of learning and privilege. Among other sources, the *Malleus Maleficarium* details the various ways in which its authors believed men could participate in magic [2], and as Ankarloo, Bengt and Hennigsen note, "Most of the people accused in Finland were men, so called "wise men" hired to perform magic by people." [3] Indeed, even during the infamous Salem Witch Trials, six of the twenty-five victims – and many of the accused – were men.

~~ ~~ ~~ ~~

This essay, then, hopes to relocate the practice and possibility of a masculine magical craft which exists outside of – or in complex relationship to – structures of power and privilege, in the same way that the identities of witch and cunning woman have been used to create revolutionary and restorative models of womanhood. It seeks also to explore why these methods of magical masculinity have been broadly denigrated and abandoned, and permitted to exist only in a sub-textual, half-occluded way.

---

2   For further reading, see Apps & Now, 'Literally unthinkable? Demonological descriptions of male witches' Male Witches in Early Modern Europe, www.manchesteropenhive.com/view/9781526137500/9781526137500.00009. xml, 2018

3   Ankarloo, Bengt & Henningsen, Gustav (ed.), Skrifter. Bd 13, *Häxornas Europa 1400-1700: historiska och antropologiska studier*, Stockholm, Nerenius & Santérus, 1987

*"You're a funny sod," he said. "You'd beat me to a pulp; then
cry over a dead mouse. Can't you bear to kill anything?"
"Yeah, murdering sods who go round torturing innocent
creatures for a laugh. I could stand killing a lot of them."
He studied me for a long time, not scared, just weighing me
up. "I think you really would, John. You'll do; you'll do." [4]*

In Robert Westall's *The Devil on the Road*, motorcycle
enthusiast and engineering student John Webster follows
"Lady Chance", tossing a coin to determine his route. It is this
invitation to fate which leads him to a remote Suffolk village
where the long and troubled legacy of the witch-hunts await
him. Cast in to the role of the "Cunning" by the villagers, he
is the unwilling recipient of their largesse and petitions for
assistance as he slowly realizes he has been summoned to avert
a crime three hundred years in the past: the execution a young
woman accused by Matthew Hopkins – the Yarb Mother.

As a doubly closeted transgender teenager, Webster offered
me a fascinating model of masculinity, one which embodied
certain stereotypes and assumptions around masculinity,
without being able to participate in the privilege or communities
associated with them. Educated without being an academic,
he plays rugby without feeling much fellowship to his fellow
sportsmen, and studies Civil Engineering only to be patronized
by students in more scholarly disciplines. Although he gets
involved in several fights, Webster is a reluctant warrior –
and is at his most vehement against thugs, racists and animal
cruelty. Indeed, throughout the novel, the reader is presented
with various modes of masculinity – the intellectual, the wild
biker, the football hooligan, the country squire, the lover,
the military man – and shown Webster's silent withdrawal
or exclusion from all of them. What defines him is a mixture
of tenderness and aloofness – a man who will use violence to
rescue a kitten, but is disgusted by the mere thought of

---

4   Westall, ibid, p122

warfare; who is clearly attractive and attracted to women, but is only ever seen declining sex.

It is this ambivalence to masculinity and social power that makes Webster so appropriate as both a conduit for a power beyond the villagers' control, and a vessel for their ancestral guilt. As there is no possible identity through which he could be "one of them", he is able to exist outside the community and, in a strange exile, bear the weight of both their gratitude and condemnation.

It is a part he plays long before arriving in Suffolk and a dangerous position to occupy. Webster is acutely aware of his vulnerability and how easily his rootless Otherness could open him up to accusations of criminality, to exploitation, violence and sexual assault.

There is something emasculate about using magic or other unseen arts to solve your problems, something suspicious about having knowledge that other people do not – and any knowledge that is instinctive to some is given the weight of mystery by those to whom it is not.

Perhaps that is why ceremonial magicians vouchsafe so much to text, to initiation, to recorded information – why the earliest scientists were alchemists, too [5]. The information may be secret, but it is information that codifies itself for posterity, even if only for fellow initiates, the peers in a stratified system that mimics the wider, political world [6].

Folk magic, though, is responsive rather than learned; resistant to empirical testing, it is based on the thousand subtle cues of specific time and place. It's about passion, about knack

---

5   See: Maxwell-Stuart, P G, *The Chemical Choir: a History of Alchemy*, Continuum, 2012.
6   An example of a magical tradition of this sort is the ritual included in *The Book of Abramelin the Mage*, Abraham, et al. *The Book of Abramelin a New Translation*, Ibis Press, 2015.

– sniffing the wind and tasting rain, trick shots taken with no formal study of calculus, knowing in the minute tensile shifts felt beneath your fingers when the dough has been kneaded enough. It is a craft that can be grown untaught, or passed from hand to hand – not merely learned. You can only really explain to someone else who has the air on their lips, the gun in their hands, the dough between their fingers. It is tactile, intimate and somehow intangible – a quality of inquiry, of attention paid.

"Folk magic, though, is responsive rather than learned"

What is more, people are resistant to learning it. In my own experience as a cook, I have found people are stubborn in their ignorance – surely bread does not need an oven that hot, surely the pastry needs more working and the eggs less, and it is not possible I mean to use that much butter. They do not want a chemist but a magic worker, who pulls off the trick by some innate virtue that cannot be replicated through mundane means.

Thus, while Webster's actions are always pragmatic, his study, his observant nature and his access to information outside the local norm condemns him to strangeness – whether that strangeness is his use of anachronistic technology in the seventeenth century, or giving an antibiotic soap to a rural girl coming to "The Cunning" for a mystical acne cure. Yet while people might exclaim in wonder at the result, such unwonted knowledge always creates an invisible line between the knower and those to whom the knowledge is revealed, and Webster is immediately uncomfortable with the village's acclaim.

Perhaps that is because receiving intangible knowledge requires a degree of openness, a certain passivity. It is the holding of the dowsing rods in the hand, waiting for them to twitch; the opening of your mind to the tarot cards as the meaning clears itself; the gentle silence that allows the skies to speak. To receive, you must be receptive on the very level of the body and in that regard it is a queer act, one at odds with conventional modes of cis, straight masculinity.

Most of the cis men I know who practise some form of folk magic – rather than, or in addition to, ceremonial magic – are brusque about it to the point of embarrassment, unwilling to dwell on the mechanism. It's a trick, a knack, a self-evident thing. You either understand it, they imply, or you do not. There's no need to go in to too much detail, we all know how these things work.

The fact you are listening tends to mean that you do.

In this way, the transmission of folk knowledge among men forms a current that is not so much occult as implicit: a coding that remains invisible except to those to whom it is directed. In such ways it transmits itself under the radar of authority and outsiders – a secret tongue of assumed understanding – like thieves' cant or the hanky codes of the United States. Most of all, it disowns itself – "Don't get the wrong idea," it tries to say, "I'm not really in to this, it's just that sometimes ..."

─── ─── ─── ───

This metaphorical relation between magic and bodily receiving finds its literal expression through the bodies of trickster deities like Loki, whose fluidity of form and moral status are crucial parts of his magics. A shapeshifter and a crossdresser, Loki's body both penetrates and is penetrated: he is open to the world – to ideas, to solutions, to trickery, to penetration, and – significantly – to pregnancy [7].

It is only through this openness that he has access to knowledge that most men (and certainly the cis ones) will never know – the dangerous, magical and externally unknowable experience of childbearing. In my experience, pregnancy and childbirth are the

---

7   For details of Loki's appearances in mythology, see Rooth, Anna Birgitta, *Loki in Scandinavian Mythology*, C W K Gleerup, 1961

real sticking point for any expanded definition of masculinity. Crucial to my own transition was the long held and socially endorsed assumption that pregnancy would "fix" me in to womanhood, and the emotional crisis that resulted when it did not. Indeed, even if a person is willing to accept the theoretical existence of transmasculine people, they are often drawn up short by the idea that we might remain men even when we have had – or wish to have – children. In an argument online some years ago, I was told that Dr James Barry could not possibly have been a trans man, because he had given birth, as though that sole act negated his name, his life, his dying wish to be known as a man.

Meanwhile, I had given birth twice and still wasn't a woman.

This assumption that the pregnant body, the penetrated body, is an anathema to masculinity is widespread – and one which Luce Irigaray expresses when she writes of contemporary, capitalist masculinity as being an indivisible singular, an impermeable, irreducible "one" [8]. It is in that image of internally complete wholeness that I feel the prevailing cultural view of masculinity is best expressed – something impenetrable, complete unto itself, and separate from the world around it.

By contrast, the feminine body is perceived as an irreducible difference, an unknowable and inexpressible space that holds a form of creation inaccessible to masculinity. In that space, unknown magics and mechanisms take place, which are difficult to verify externally: ovulation, menstrual cramps, g-spot orgasms, PMT, hot flushes, the quickening of a pregnancy.

Yet this space is identical to the space in which instinctive magic occurs, where – through unseen, unknowable mechanisms – we allow power to grow within ourselves, and birth it in order to alter the world.

---

8   Irigaray, Luce, *This Sex Which Is Not One*, Cornell University Press, 1977, p.23

Discursively, that power is feminine, yes – but its true disruptive potential is that it is open to all of us, and in being so, it challenges the cultural hegemony of the masculine "one" and the social power attendant upon it. It lets us know that masculinity, any masculinity, is not whole unto itself, and can have space opened up within it for strangeness and wonder to be born. This existential threat to masculinity is so severe that all men who indulge in such practices place themselves under immediate suspicion. Because any power that works unknowably is a power that exercises itself outside of the constraints of the social structures surrounding masculine honour and status. If one is prepared to let oneself be penetrated – literally or discursively – what else might one do?

～～ ～～ ～～ ～～

This fear is key to Loki's power. Through his unfixed form and outsider status among the Æsir, he is able to access places and information that are unavailable to the other gods – to play endless roles, both benevolent and malicious. Because of his "openness", there are no secrets beyond him, no disguises he cannot wear, no knacks he cannot master, no problem he cannot solve – or create. Yet Loki is not the only male magic worker in the Norse pantheons.

Odin is also a shape-shifter. The patriarchal image of Odin – drawn up by Victorians and appropriated by fascists [9] – serves our social myths of masculinity very well. He is the grand King, all knowing, all seeing, the perfect representation of Teutonic manhood. Or else, he is a bloodstained and brutal throwback to some "savage" past, a past only tamed and tempered – or castrated, depending on your prejudices – by the "civilizing" influence of Christianity.

---

9 For more on this, see: Junginger, Horst. *The Study of Religion under the Impact of Fascism*, Brill, 2008, p556 and McKinnell, John. *Meeting the Other in Norse Myth and Legend*, Boydell & Brewer, 2017, p32

Praised or denigrated, Odin is familiar to us all as a warrior or King, but my own experiences as a devotee of the Allfather has been that of Godhead crying out upon the World Tree for the secrets that bind the universe together, Godhead penetrated by his own spear, whose mouth births runic truths, and inside whose mind the very shape of thought alters, silent and unseen[10].

Odin is paradox made divinity: his ability to hold the larger picture, the longer workings within him, place him apart from the specifics of his time. This is an elevation, yes, but it is also a burden. Keeping the hall of Valhalla, he draws the finest warriors to him, yet he himself sits apart on Hlidskjalf or wanders the Nine Worlds as Grimnir – the masked one. He is the Allfather, making treaties and bringing peace, and he is Glad of War, revelling in its brutal toll. Yet beneath this contradiction lies another, and then another still – for the splendour and hospitality of Valhalla are all to serve the battle of Ragnarok, and the gladness for war is only to bring the finest warriors to that place – that he might hope to preserve the fragile beauty of light and learning, which that battle will destroy. And underlying it all, is the long, hard reality of true knowledge that all this work, this paradox, this preparation is doomed to fail.

Thus, working beyond and around ordinary understanding, conventional emotion, Odin cannot be perfectly perceived – he is hooded, masked, indeterminate. He exists in the very space that permits instinctive magic, and is rendered dangerous, suspect because of it. His foreknowledge and insight become omens of misfortune, or even acts of malice – such as in the ballad Earl Brand [11] where he appears as "old Carl Hood," and shares the truths that leads the eponymous hero to disaster.

---

10 For the myths of Odin's death and rebirth, see Bray, Oliver, *The Elder or Poetic Edda; Commonly Known as Saemunds Edda*. Edited and Translated with Introd. and Notes by Olve Bray. Illustrated by W G Collingwood, printed for the Viking Club, 1908, p105

11 Traditional, "Earl Brand" from *The Oxford Book of Ballads*, ed. Quiller-Couch, 190, p157–160

~~~ ~~~ ~~~ ~~~

This is the dangerous edge walked by any practitioner of folk magic – or any who have knowledge that is hidden. What is the difference between foretelling disaster and causing it? If the mechanism is hidden within you, secret and unknown, who is to say your prediction was not a curse, that with the power of your words you did not speak tragedy into being?

Indeed, the idea of foreknowledge being a blight or curse is one very commonly associated with the folk witch, a fear which Webster expresses in his novel, *The Devil on the Road*. When he expresses disdain for a motorcycle engine or driver, is he laying an ill will upon them? Or is he merely revealing a Gift which goes against conventional Western understandings of masculinity: knowledge without ability to effect change? No longer a virile actor within events, but a too-wise observer of them.

If I'd made love to her, I knew I'd be part of everything forever, rooted in the stones and bones of dead men. And that turned me stone dead. Every time.[12]

More than mere passivity, this knowledge – or sometimes the push against the inevitable effects of this knowledge – has its cost. Just as birth requires a certain surrender of autonomy to an unstoppable process, all other old deep magic requires the spilling of blood, the loss of control, the offering of sacrifice. What do we bargain away for knowledge, safety, change?

Socially, maleness wants the body of Godhead – and by extension our own masculine bodies – to be inviolable, whole and unmarked. We would have ourselves masterful and golden upon the throne or else bloodied and victorious in battle. When we act magically, we wish the action to be out in the world – with any penetration involved happening to someone who is not ourselves.

---

12 Westall, ibid, p214

Yet to affect change, the world must be permitted to enter and change our bodies. Tyr sacrifices his good right hand to bind Fenrir; Osiris is castrated, his severed testicles bringing fertility to the banks of the Nile; John Barleycorn bleeds away in to the earth to assure the harvest, Adonis to bring the rain.

"When we act magically, we wish the action to be out in the world"

In *The Devil on the Road*, Webster ultimately fails because at the last minute, he refuses the cost of the magic in which he has engaged – not his life, but his surrender; the opening up of his body and his heart. He takes refuge in the logical world of mechanical and technological masculinity, fearing that the price will be too high, will sap, or kill or unman him in some crucial way.

Mythologically, the cost of such power is often the loss of the markers or privileges of 'whole' masculinity. Both Odin and Loki insult one another with their perceived effeminacy[13], while any type of disability is excluded from the discursive concept of the "ideal masculinity" – unless the injury was taken in the service of violence. Why else is it that we prefer the stories of the uninjured Thor to the disabled Tyr – and a very particular, buff and handsome Thor, at that? Why do modern pop-culture stories of the Norse gods show Odin losing his eye in battle rather than in magical bargaining[14]? We do not like to let our gods have their failings, their wounds, their penetrations.

But Odin lost his eye as he lost his life: in the pursuit of knowledge, a willing sacrifice to himself, a breaking of his body's wholeness not to prevent the catastrophe of Ragnarok, but to understand it. One must surrender to the killing blow or enact it upon oneself, one must – in the conventional sense

---

13 Bray, Oliver, *The Elder or Poetic Edda; Commonly Known as Saemunds Edda*, printed for the Viking Club, 1908, p255
14 For example, *Thor*, Marvel Studios, Paramount Pictures, 2011

– lose, accepting that one cannot engage in these magics while remaining the unmarked, unpenetrated Irigrian "one".

It is significant, also, that it is Odin's eye he loses. Freud, having a field day with the myth of Oedipus, would doubtless draw the same conclusion about the symbolic significance of this partial-blinding – done not in remorse, but in pursuit of knowledge he cannot have without symbolic partial-castration. The devotees of Cybele knew the same truths: some knowledge, some magical power is not available to those unwilling to put aside the mantle of manhood. Odin himself sought the knowledge of seið – a witchcraft traditionally associated with women[15], and there are some (disputed) statues such as the Odin of Lejre, which show him in traditionally feminine garb[16].

This is not to say that such power is female, in any essentialist sense of the word. It is rather to say that it is feminine insofar as it lies outside the scope of the culturally masculine, and is forbidden to men without cost – be that of honour, of dignity, of respect. It is to recognize that our masculinities are a construct, and an inadequate one at that, one that does not let our bodies be vulnerable – to injury, to failure, to emotion; nor to be open – to magic, to penetration, to change.

Yet, in the paradoxical nature of Odin, simply to say that those modes are inadequate does not mean we must abandon them entirely. For unlike the Priests of Cybele – who assumed a female role full time and arguably could be described as trans women, Odin remains the sacred but penetrated masculine – and bears both the honour and shame of it. Indeed, it is his very deconstruction and disregard for the stern boundaries of

15 For some excellent perspectives on this, see Blain, Jenny, *Nine Worlds of Seid-Magic: Ecstasy and Neo-Shamanism in North European Paganism,* Routledge, Taylor & Francis Group, 2002 and Paxson, Diana L, "Drumming with the witches, Odin and Women's Wisdom", https://hrafnar.org/articles/dpaxson/norse/odin-women/, first published 1998

16 Christensen, Tom, "Odin fra Lejre", ROMU, 2009, Årsskrift fra Roskilde Museum (in Danish). Roskilde: Roskilde Museum: pp6–26

maleness that elevate him, and make him the Allfather – just
as it is his knowledge of the boundaries of the time of the
gods that renders that time so precious to him, and places him
foremost within it.

What does this mean for our practice? It means that we
should not be like John Webster – so afraid of death, of
penetration, of emasculation – that we run in fear from
the possibility of true connection with the world, seeking
instead to crush it beneath our will. Instead, we look to Odin
as he reveals to us a manhood that transcends manhood; a
masculinity that exists in the spaces outside those sanctioned
for masculinity; a masculinity that recognizes the boundaries
between itself and the world are permeable, and that inviolate
wholeness serves only to isolate us from true knowledge,
magic and insight. It is a masculinity that is complex, suspect,
paradoxical – one that is open to possibility and all the magics
of the world.

THE FIRST
RULE OF
WITCH CLUB

"There's a strange silence surrounding the cattiness, in-fighting, dramatics, backstabbing and mudslinging (both virtual and magical) among witches."

7

THE FIRST RULE OF WITCH CLUB

BY SABRINA SCOTT

Note from the editors: *We had the pleasure of interviewing writer and witch Sabrina Scott, whose experience in, and expertise on, the occult online communities made us curious. Here, they talk about the idea of witch club, and answer some questions about what it means to be online as a witch in the twenty-first century, and how we can build different, more positive online communities.*

THE FIRST RULE OF WITCH CLUB IS YOU DON'T TALK ABOUT WITCH CLUB.

One thing I've learned in my two decades of practising magic – and engaging with others who do too – is that people in the witchcraft community love to fight. With each other, on the internet. This includes your favs, your heroes, your friends, leaders in your community and maybe even you.

THE SECOND RULE OF WITCH CLUB IS YOU DON'T TALK ABOUT WITCH CLUB.

And nobody talks about it.

There's a strange silence surrounding the cattiness, in-fighting, dramatics, backstabbing and mudslinging (both virtual and magical) among witches.

It's pervasive, and I've seen it all, from incredibly defensive and hostile social media wars inspired by negative online reviews left on a witchy shop, to people seeking to be the witchy head-honcho of their community and viciously demolishing (with gossip, rumours, malice, whatever) the reputation of any competition, to ridiculous social media ass-kissing in public (and smack-talking in private) in order to ladder-climb. I've seen this among teens, practitioners in their fifties, newbies and experienced folk alike.

Of course, most people are kinda assholes. I guess that's true.

But on the other hand, I also believe that the world is full of absolutely lovely, sincere, genuine people who are an absolute pleasure to get to know. And I believe this is true whether or not we believe the same things, practise in the same way. Human decency still exists, even if we have a different idea of what witchcraft is. So does the possibility for mutual respect, mutual curiosity – even mutual ignoring, when that's the best option. Or, at least, it should.

THE THIRD RULE OF WITCH CLUB IS IF SOMEONE YELLS "STOP!", GOES LIMP OR TAPS OUT, KEEP FIGHTING.

As a person for whom witchcraft has always been about relationships (with the self, with plants, animals, skyscrapers, the soil, the lake, coffee cups, pizza boxes, spirits, divinities, lighters and everything in between), I'm perpetually taken aback by the almost impossibility of escaping the seemingly unending fight dynamics of witch club. Someone seems genuinely hurt? Great, blame them. Better yet, get defensive, send a nasty message, insult their personality, their appearance and whatever divinity they work with. Don't stop 'til you get blocked seems to be the rule – and even then, I've been on the receiving end even after I've blocked multiple accounts.

THE FOURTH RULE OF WITCH CLUB IS TO GET AS MANY PEOPLE TO GANG UP ON YOUR TARGET AS YOU CAN.

What disappoints me so much about this is that the witchcraft community is often where people go to meet themselves, the world, the spirits and others more deeply, to heal – from trauma, from mental health challenges, from feeling ineffective in their own lives, from loneliness and ostracism. And, unfortunately, folks seeking accepting, healthy social groups bound together by a shared love and devotion to witchcraft often find something that looks a little like the opposite of peace, healing, coexistence and growth. I'd call that something "harm". And it's often collectively inflicted.

THE FIFTH RULE OF WITCH CLUB IS TO GANG UP ON A FEW PEOPLE AT A TIME AND THEN MOVE ON.

I've had people threaten to sue me, extort me; I've had people create group chats to harass me, coordinating their flood into my inbox whenever I posted. I've had people make memes of my face, make up untrue things about me, who I am, what I believe and what I do, and share them all over various social media platforms. Why? For being a person on the internet who has opinions about witchcraft and tarot.

I'm not sharing this to get pity, sympathy, or to claim victimhood: I'm sharing this because I know I'm not special; I know this is happening to so many other people in the community. I share this because it ain't about me; there's something systemic happening here in the wider culture, especially among witches online.

THE SIXTH RULE OF WITCH CLUB IS THAT YOUR VULNERABILITY WILL BE USED AS AMMUNITION FOR AN ATTACK.

I know witchcraft isn't the same thing for everyone – and thank god for that, it shouldn't be. I love the diversity of this practice. For some folks, witchcraft means atheism and praying to their holy dead, lighting candles, doing ritual; for others the most important thing is an unyielding ritual devotion to the divine; for others still it's more about tapping into ancestral practices of magic and connection with the land. It's all of this, and more; and more.

And yet, somehow, despite the beauty and power of this thing we all have in common, our witchy community – if it can be called that – has largely lost its way. As a whole, we've become so concerned with aesthetic, clout, followers and being at the top of a hierarchy (of something that is, let's not forget, wildly fringe), that we've forgotten how to be people. And we've forgotten that other people are people, too – with their own bad days, triggers, traumas, confusions, joys and hopes. We're all big children in a small sandbox and we've forgotten how to share our toys.

THE SEVENTH RULE OF WITCH CLUB IS THAT THE FIGHT WILL GO ON AS LONG AS IT HAS TO.

I'd like to see a different kind of "witch club" – one that isn't so privy to fighting, social media wars and thinly veiled scarcity and desperation dynamics masquerading as, well … something else. It's like we've forgotten that magic makes all things possible. Are we really so afraid of the ineffectiveness of our magic that we resort to acting as though there is barely enough (love, happiness, money, success, healing, confidence) for any of us?

There's enough for all of us to succeed, whatever that means to us – whether we'd rather focus on succeeding at our personal practice and rolling deep with our spiritual team and our devotion to ritual, or whether we've moved into a space of sharing our expertise and knowledge with others.

THE EIGHTH RULE OF WITCH CLUB IS IF IT'S YOUR FIRST TIME AT WITCH CLUB, YOU HAVE TO FIGHT.

I'd like to see a witch club where instead of bickering with each other and slinging mud online – or even dragging one another publicly – we simply divest our attention from folks whose work and ways of being don't resonate. I'd like to see a community where we find the folks we vibe with and build each other up, rather than publicly tearing down people whose personalities, relationship with money or style of practice we don't like.

I'd like to see a witch club based on the idea that all of this isn't about establishing our superiority over anyone else. I'd like to see a community where folks don't feel like they have to become educators and publish books in order to be respected and seen as relevant.

Instead of a witch club where people talk shit and attempt to annihilate total strangers for no reason, I'd like to see a community where people are confident enough in themselves and their own magic – and the life it can help them create – that they aren't threatened by the success (or even the existence) of others, magical or otherwise.

I'd like to see a witch club where folks don't just copy each other, thinking that's the only way to be valid or succeed. I'd like to see a community where we collectively accept and elevate innovations and new ideas, even if it's something we've never done in our own practice.

Witchcraft and magic can be a way for folks who feel powerless to regain their power.

That's not all it is, obviously; this can be a beautiful and productive process. So maybe that's why this behaviour is such a problem in our communities, especially online: a lot of folks look to practise magic in order to create change, in themselves and in their lives. It's a way to gain some semblance of control in an otherwise chaotic world. I get that; I came to witchcraft during the most chaotic and traumatic time of my life. So maybe witchy spaces have a large proportion of people who feel somehow powerless. Fighting online is certainly one way to regain a lost sense of power. It is, after all, a way to create change in accordance with will – being a complete and utter asshole is a quick way to inspire outrage, discord and drama.

This behaviour disturbs me because it's largely people in their thirties participating: people who, by anyone's estimation, should know better. Not just as people, but as witches. The most effective magic I've found has been the workings I've done on myself: to curb my bad habits, to steer myself toward better coping mechanisms, to clear the road ahead of me and ensure my movements will be smooth. People like to mud sling at everyone in their vicinity, but it's often ourselves that are the biggest impediment to our success. Magic to control and influence others does work, but I find it often misses the point.

These online arguers have missed one of the most important and transformative lessons of magic: eyes on your own page.

Turning inward creates ripples; self-work is community work.

When we're right with ourselves, all of our relationships and interactions transform.

Our lives change.

This is magic.

I would love to see what else we can dream, what else we can magic into being: something that isn't just people feeling threatened, afraid, insecure, ashamed, whatever and projecting that rage into someone who didn't cause it (at least, not really).

I'd love us to collectively move as though we believe magic is real, that abundance is possible, that joy, growth and sincerity are worth fighting for.

I don't really want a witch club.

I want a community.

_____ _____ _____ _____

We were lucky enough to be able to delve deeper with Sabrina into the intricacies behind this bold manifesto.

What is it about the online occult community, do you think, that creates the conditions for hostility?

So I do think this an "online in general right now" kind of thing, and of course occult and witchy spaces are absolutely no exception. That being said, I am in online spaces where this kind of dynamic doesn't really happen, and so I think there is something specific and interesting about occult spaces and the way this behaviour occurs there.

We are slowly coming out of a global pandemic, a once-per-century event (hopefully), and so a lot of the west – the space I myself am in – has been largely "extremely online," as they say. This is a real concept, "extremely online" – which has been described as a bit of a fandom without the ... typical things associated with fandom, like a show or series.

Being online was the only type of social interaction available to many of us, or at least those of us with particular risk assessments, myself included.

All of this of course influences occult online spaces.

Occult online spaces, I think, do tend to include many folks who feel or are marginalized – occultism, of course, is one way of accessing and reclaiming power for people who may feel powerless for a variety of reasons. I know it was for me, as an eight-year-old trapped at home dealing with child abuse. So, I get that. Magic and witchcraft saved my life many times over, when many institutional resources were absolutely toothless in advocating for me and my safety. So trust me, I get the power of this practice as a way of healing and reconnecting to our agency and ability to create the lives we want. That's my story, after all.

And yet I do think sometimes this large volume of marginalized identities – and sometimes an excess focus on that – can mean that the occult community can have many of the same problems as the social justice community does. Occult community can very much be, who can be the biggest fish in the small pond? This is another way the discomfort with powerlessness – and the desire for power – can manifest. At its worst, this ethos creates nasty cult leaders and even just unhealthy power-hungry coven governesses. I've seen that play out so many times. Wherever there's people, there will be conflict. And when multiple people are desperately grappling for power – to be the lead king or queen or ruler of the very tiny occult sandbox – hostility can happen. I find it incredibly sad. The impact of this is often that wounded newbies with high hopes, good intentions and the desire for support, often end up even more wounds, this time inflicted by the community they turned to for solace.

It sounds like it perhaps wasn't always thus ... how did you find your way into the online witchcraft world? In spite of the difficulties, what benefits are there to being online as a witchcraft practitioner?

It wasn't always like this, that's for sure!

When I first got online in the late 1990s, the internet was a lot less visual. I engaged with fellow practitioners on message boards, in long and drawn-out debates and conversations. We all used aliases, and though we did many gift exchanges, none of us really shared photos of ourselves or our practices. We taught each other new techniques, discussed metaphysics and cosmology and belief, we troubleshooted one anothers' workings to see what might have influenced an unsuccessful ritual to transpire as it had. There was a lot less of an emphasis on ego and positioning oneself prematurely as a teacher or expert. We built these genuine online relationships and connections with one another over time, and it wasn't really about power or showing off or building any cult following. I miss that genuine conversation and learning, and those spaces do in some ways inspire the kinds of vibes I want to cultivate in my online course spaces: I want to create containers where everyone is welcomed in their own uniqueness, and encouraged to get their hands messy and report back. That's where all the fun and breakthroughs happen, and it's also how people learn and gain confidence in their practice.

It was the age before Facebook, before social media. Weirdly it wasn't too hard to find my way – I found some good message boards and list servs. As a young kiddo living in the middle of nowhere (Bible Town USA, more specifically), the internet was where I connected with people with similar interests. Weirdly, I remember absolutely no nastiness or bullying. Everyone was good to me, despite knowing almost nothing about me.

Now, the best thing about being online is I get to create the change I want to see. I always tell folks the only failed spell I've ever done was one to find a witchy community in my early-mid 20s. The candle just wouldn't stay lit. So I built my own community of amazing people through my social media presence on Instagram, and through the private community spaces I make available to students of my Magic Without Bullshit and Tarot Without Bullshit courses. There are rules, and there's a culture that supports vulnerability, realness and mutual support. I love the work I do, I love being able to share my ideas online, I love being able to teach students and connect with clients from all around the world, from France to Australia to Dubai to India to the UK to the USA to Canada. Without the internet, I wouldn't be able to work across time and place. It's the best.

Your essay notes that both the first and second rules of witch club are not to talk about witch club. Why do you think there is such a disinclination to speak up about – and attempt to reinvent – our occult communities?

Well, I think it goes back to the basic psychology of belonging. We all want to belong. Often, to not belong can mean death – whether psychic or physical. Community ostracism and rejection can feel like one of the worst betrayals. Sometimes folks come to witchcraft and the occult looking for community and kinship because maybe they don't feel like they "fit in" with regular society or family, however you want to define that. It can feel shameful and embarrassing to admit to someone else that we've been or felt rejected, or we've been the target of harassment, abuse or even just weirdness. I think sometimes people don't talk about witch club because they're afraid that in talking about it, they'll have that position of rejection reified and consolidated rather than challenged. Sometimes people can distance themselves from victims of abuse or mistreatment; it is like we are thought to be contagious, lepers.

And I think this is part of why we see so many mass pile-ons happening, both in occult space, in social justice space and online in general. I remember a year or so ago there was a mass harassment campaign against me led by some teenagers who were race-shifting (basically, white teens pretending not to be white, and then crying racism at anyone around them). In hindsight the whole thing was laughably ridiculous, but one thing that surprised me was that one girl who I'd gone to undergrad with – and therefore known for like a decade – also chose to join in and pile on me, totally swindled by these charlatans in her desire to distance herself from whoever was declared "bad" that day, lest she be thought to be associated with badness. It didn't upset me; I'm always happy to see someone's true colours, but it taught me a lot about her character and the basics of human psychology. Given a choice between truth and giving into fear, most people will give into the fear and enact violence or ostracism against others, so long as it means they themselves will be safe from violence or even simple rejection.

In the last part of the essay you say you want to feel less like witchcraft is a club, and more like it's a community. What would your ideal witchcraft community look like?

Honestly, I feel like this would likely involve an overhaul of internet culture. I'd like to see fewer people focused on self-declaring expertise after practising only for a year. I'd like to see more critical thinking, more actual reading of books, more of people getting their hands and feet and bodies dirty. I'd like to see people build spiritual skills and share what they've learned. I'd like to see more questions, fewer statements. I'd honestly like to see less posturing and fewer medieval outfits, but hey, that's just a personal preference, lol.

Wherever you go, there you are. Self-work is community work. Our communities are really only as strong, thoughtful, compassionate self-aware and able to withstand healthy conflict, as we are as individuals. People are confusing boring-ass normative conflict with the violence of abuse. Tolerance of discomfort is seriously so low right now. All of this needs to change, we all need to work on ourselves – and be okay with working through some of this in the context of our relationships with other people. In collectives, in classes, online, in community. Community isn't always safe, but it can be brave. Community is a space we can trust to catch us. Real community means real relationships, means we're not afraid of being discarded for the most minute misstep. Community means we can hold space for our differences, for conflict, for disagreement, for questions, for curiosity. It means we can be okay with not everyone and everything being for us. It means personal responsibility and realizing we can't (and shouldn't want to) control others. Community is messy sometimes and it ain't always easy, but it is worth our time to build.

What I see right now is a lot of mean girls (and guys, and nonbinary folks) fixated on scarcity and acting badly. There is truly enough room for all of us. I really do believe that.

What concrete steps do you think we – as participants in online witchcraft culture – can each take to help make this community a reality? What needs to be done, on an individual and on a collective level?

Stop being whiny c**ts at each other.

That sounds rude, but for real – I do think that's a big part of it. So many people get sucked into these relational dynamics – talking shit, responding to shit, gossiping, paying attention to people who we hate, sharing screen caps. You don't like what someone's doing? Cool. Use that as inspiration to make your own point, to create your own content, your own writing and art – without tearing someone else down. Divest from what you don't like. Stop following and watching the social media of folks you love to hate in the community, whether out of jealousy or lack of respect. Spend time creating, not destroying.

Of course, there is a time to ask questions. I got called a mentally-ill, hysterical woman for having the audacity to wonder out loud about the vetting process for so-called occult experts at an online event. To say that wasn't received well was an understatement. I learned a lot from that situation:

1. Go where you're wanted, desired and respected.
2. Notice how people respond when questioned or denied. If they're rude and pop off, that's crucial data. Do you want to be around someone like that?
3. Pay attention to whether people are in it for clout and connections or genuine interest. How do they treat people who can do nothing for them?
4. You can't persuade people to respect you if they are committed to not doing so.
5. You can't control whether or not someone is open and curious. Move with the curious folks.
6. Spend time and energy with people who can hear you and who want to hear you.
7. If someone is being nasty, don't persuade – divest.
8. No one owes you a relationship, and you don't owe anyone a relationship. Move accordingly.
9. Spend time with people and in spaces that feel expansive, not constrictive.
10. If you feel like you're walking on eggshells or that your acceptance by the group is predicated on you toeing a party line – think about whether or not this is really a psychologically supportive place to be.

One of the most important things I've done to help create this sense of healthy community is to spend time on what's positive and beautiful – my own courses, my own social media, my own students and clients, and encouraging all of that to blossom and bloom. I look toward that and look decidedly away from everything else. I unfollowed most people in the occult and witchy space, because I stopped respecting how they moved.

Instead of trying to change them and their idea of community, I changed myself and my own behaviour by removing myself from spaces these people frequented and created. I didn't like the culture and community they cultivated, so I stopped paying attention to it and started putting so much more of myself in what *did* and *does* feel good to me – and that means moving in a completely different way.

In the book *Counterpublics*, Michael Warner writes that a counterpublic isn't just a public that is "against" or "anti" something – that's just another public. A true counterpublic defines itself via creation – by cultivating movement, being, and belonging in a completely new and beautiful way. Let's be that. Be the change, create the change that you want to see. Don't take no for an answer and dream big. It is possible.

Are there any resources you can signpost less experienced practitioners to? Especially ones that you think embody good ethics and practice!

I'd say that every book you read is a book about witchcraft, if you know how to read it.

Read widely. Not just religious studies and works on the occult, but psychology, family and relationship dynamics, cult dynamics, environmental studies, philosophy and whatever else strikes your fancy. Follow your bliss. That's where the magic lives.

WITCHCRAFT, INDIGENOUS RELIGION AND THE ETHICS OF DECOLONIZATION

"The relationship between contemporary witchcraft and indigenous religion is ambiguous ..."

8

WITCHCRAFT, INDIGENOUS RELIGION AND THE ETHICS OF DECOLONIZATION: AN EXPERIMENT IN CO-LABOURING

BY SIMONE KOTVA

*T*he relationship between contemporary witchcraft and indigenous religion is ambiguous and points toward urgent ethical questions, but ones that remain largely neglected, especially in books aimed at practitioners. Most of those practitioners, like myself, identify as Western and were not raised in an indigenous culture. At the same time, many practitioners – again, like myself – may be attempting to reconnect with indigenous ancestry or else experience a spiritual affinity with indigenous religions. How to reconnect and express that affinity respectfully, in a way that would result in communication rather than heightened conflict? Marisol de la Cadena, an anthropologist who has written about the encounter between Western spirituality and contemporary Amerindian religion, calls this kind of generative communication between different spiritual cultures "co-labouring."[1] What I want to do in this chapter is think through what co-labouring looks like in the case of contemporary witchcraft and indigeneity.

---

1   Cadena, Marisol de la, *Earth Beings: Ecologies of Practice Across Andean Worlds*, Durham, Duke University Press, 2015

For the contemporary witchcraft practitioner who identifies as Western, the first step toward co-labouring is recognizing that the history of modern witchcraft is inseparable from the history of colonialism. On the one hand, and in contrast to certain other contemporary attitudes, the quest for magic recognizes few cultural or ethnic barriers. Practitioners who identify as witches today typically value indigenous religions highly and consider them seriously. On the other hand, though, modern witchcraft was created by Westerners and has a long history of appropriating aspects of indigenous religions to validate the authenticity of its own practices and beliefs. Gerald Gardner (1884–1964), the founding figure of the modern witchcraft revival, botanized freely among the local religions he encountered during his years working for the rubber tree plantation industry in Borneo and Malaysia. In the 1980s and '90s – the period that I'll be focusing on in this chapter – many books aimed at practitioners claimed that witchcraft was – if not identical with – then certainly equivalent to indigenous religion. For example, Doreen Valiente (one of Gardner's first initiates and an early and influential authority on witchcraft) argued that contemporary witchcraft was a "return to shamanism pure and simple."[2] Scott Cunningham, in *Wicca: A Guide to the Solitary Practitioner* (1989), a book that remains popular among practitioners and opened witchcraft to a wider public, defined witchcraft simply as "a shamanic religion."[3] Similar equivalences between witchcraft, European paganism and shamanism are found in the prominent work of Janet and Stewart Farrar, Vivianne Crowley and many others.[4]

---

2 Valiente, Doreen, *The Rebirth of Witchcraft*, Hale, 1989, p193, cf. p65
3 Cunningham, Scott, *Wicca: A Guide for the Solitary Practitioner*, Woodbury: Llewellyn, 2004 (1989), p4, see also pp3-8
4 See for example, Janet and Stewart Farrar, *The Witches' Way*, reprinted in *The Witches' Bible*, pp194-195 (who refer to "pagan shamanistic practices" in order to authenticate features of modern witchcraft), and Vivianne Crowley, *Wicca: A Comprehensive Guide to the Old Religion in the Modern World*, HarperCollins, 2003 (first published 1996), Chapter 3 (where Crowley likewise traces modern witchcraft to "the Dionysian ecstatic and shamanistic practices of the Paganism of the woods and groves.").

These claims to indigeneity – many of which are still repeated in new books on witchcraft – took liberties with non-Western practices and are inseparable from Western interpretations and projections. The "shamanism" invoked by witchcraft authors in the 1980s and '90s does not refer to the practice of the *šaman*, the religious specialist of the Tungusic peoples of Siberia. During the eighteenth and nineteenth centuries, and as a result of colonialism, accounts of the Tungusic *šaman* were romanticized by Western scholars and drawn on to buttress theories of an "original," "archaic" religion presumed to exist among all indigenous peoples regardless of particular cultural context.[5] In the 1960s, "shamanism" became popular in the pagan and witchcraft environment where the shaman was seen not only as an indigenous religious specialist but as an ability latent in all humans.[6] Two books were important in popularizing this concept of shamanism among witchcraft authors. The first was Mircea Eliade's *Shamanism: Archaic Techniques of Ecstasy* (1953), which introduced shamanism as an ancient mystical practice surviving among indigenous peoples and ripe for "discovery" by Westerners. The other was Michael Harner's *The Way of the Shaman: A Guide to Power and Healing* (1980), written by an anthropologist but aimed at Western spiritual seekers wanting to practice Eliade's "archaic" religion for themselves. In this context, the presentation of modern witchcraft as "shamanism" that we find in the popular books of Valiente, Cunningham and others rely on a history of colonialism and become problematic as instances of cultural appropriation and theft, but also of cultural generalization. Much like Western occultism in general, modern witchcraft in particular has been criticized for fostering an explorer's or collector's mentality – a hallmark of the very neo-colonialism its advocates so often purport to resist.

---

5   Flaherty, Gloria, *Shamanism and the Eighteenth Century*, Princeton University Press, 1992
6   Wallis, Robert J, *Shamans/Neo-Shamans: Ecstasy, alternative archaeology and contemporary Pagans*, Routledge, 2003

In light of this history, many practitioners – particularly those who, like myself, were not raised in an indigenous culture – are now wanting to decolonize witchcraft by distancing themselves from shamanism, as a mark of respect both for the culture where the term originated and for indigenous religions as such. Decolonization, which the contemporary anthropologist Deborah Bird Rose defines as the desire to "inscribe back into the world a moral presence for ourselves"[7] is today strongly felt among practitioners of witchcraft. Decolonization is debated regularly by witches in social media and online spaces, as is the concomitant task of decentring Western magical practices from European and colonial terminologies.[8] But if the desire for decolonization and decentring is evident, so too is misplaced zeal. The negative impact of misplaced zeal is also discussed regularly on social media. Among those approaching the topic from the perspective of indigeneity is Shamanic Arawak Priestess, a reader, teacher and practitioner of African traditional and indigenous religion who is also a content creator on YouTube. A number of their recent videos address the question of how witchcraft practitioners can be better allies for marginalized peoples.[9] A common way of decentring Western magical practices from colonial terminology has been to control acceptable words, a strategy sometimes referred to as "gatekeeping." In the case of witchcraft and shamanism, gatekeeping has meant calling out non-indigenous practitioners who employ "shamanism" to describe their practice without being indigenous – but it has also meant calling out anyone who identifies as a shaman.

---

7   Rose, Deborah Bird, *Reports from a Wild Country: Ethics for Decolonisation*, University of New South Wales Press, 2004, p6
8   See for example, *Talking About the Elephant: An Anthology of Neopagan Perspectives on Cultural Appropriation*, ed. Lupa, Megalithica, 2008
9   See for example, "Spirit Chat: Are You Really an Ally for Marginalized People?", 30 May 2020, www.youtube.com/watch?v=pDQ2OQmJgr0 (accessed 08 July 2021); "Spirit Chat Ways to Be an Ally and Create Change" (19 June 2020) www.youtube.com/watch?v=cmM9qtWq87M (accessed 08 July 2021)

Creators like Shamanic Arawak Priestess voice the way in which, when gatekeeping is used in this latter way, misplaced zeal shuts out indigenous practitioners who may identify as shamans for cultural and historical reasons that are ignored or deemed irrelevant to the wider discourse of decolonization.

The complexities at stake in decolonizing shamanism was the subject of a recent article by the historian of religion Konsta Kaikkonen. Kaikkonen's remarks are focused on a particular indigenous religion and its interaction with Western magic more broadly, but they have strong bearing on the subject of this chapter. Kaikkonen writes about the Sámi, the indigenous people living in Sápmi, the northern-most parts of Fenno-Scandinavia and Russia's Kola Peninsula. Kaikkonen's research wrestles with the contested phenomenon of "Sámi shamanism", which is an ambiguous phrase that may refer, on the one hand, to a colonial term for the Sámi ritual specialist (the *noaidi*), and, on the other hand, to the activities of contemporary, indigenous Sámi practitioners who identify as shamans. Because many contemporary Sámi shamans also identify as inheritors of the historical *noaidi* and work closely with received oral traditions that are linked to historical practices, it becomes important to distinguish carefully between these two meanings of "Sami shamanism" – the colonial and the indigenous. While "shamanism" is a colonial term that has nothing to do with the historical *noiadi*, among contemporary Sámi the word "shamanism" now has an indigenous history of its own – but one that is often ignored in the interest of decolonizing "Sámi shamanism."

In order to navigate the contested terrain of Sámi shamanism Kaikkonen's research traces the origins of the concept to the nineteenth century, when Finnish philologists assimilated what they knew about the *noaidi* to the then nascent paradigm of a supposed, "archaic" shamanism. Eliade included several references to the Sámi (which he refers to by their colonial name, "Lapps") in his influential book, and during the first half of the twentieth century there were many studies of Sámi religion that referred to the *noaidi* as a "shaman" and discussed Sami religion more broadly as displaying "shamanistic" characteristics. The result of this interpretation of the *noaidi*, Kaikkonen explains, was that the particular cultural context of the historical *noaidi* was neglected. Scholars like Eliade were interested in the extent to which the *noaidi* agreed with a generalized ideal of indigenous religion – they were not interested in mapping particular, local expressions of Sámi ritual practice. What is more, writers endorsing Eliade's interpretation of Sámi religion had often conducted

"What was unique to the Sámi cultrual context was either ignored or explained away"

only limited fieldwork, or none at all. As a consequence, only those aspects of the *noaidi*'s practice that "fit" the paradigm of shamanism were emphasized – at the expense of those that did not. What was unique to the Sámi cultural context was either ignored or explained away as "anomalous" deviations from an original, "archaic" shamanic religion.

Kaikkonen sees the act of discovering and testing out alternative terminology to "shamanism" as the key to decolonizing Sámi religion. "In order to recognize [the] historical baggage and come to terms with the problematic foundations of our discipline," writes Kaikkonen, "us scholars of Sámi religion must attempt to discontinue this interrogative 'Western gaze' and … [avoid] terms that are tightly knit to the exoticizing tendencies in Western academia."[10] While Kaikkonen addresses historians of religion and speaks to an academic audience of (mostly) Western scholars, their advice is applicable also to other Western-based communities wanting to decolonize shamanism – such as

---

10   Konsta Kaikkonen, "Sami indigenous(?) Religion(s)(?)— Some Observations and Suggestions Concerning Term Use," *Religions*, 2020, 11, 432, pp9-22 (p10)

practitioners of contemporary witchcraft. In place of "Sámi shamanism" Kaikkonen proposes *noaidevuohta*, a word in North Sámi that translates, roughly, as "*noaidi*-hood," or "the activities and role of the *noaidi*." Whereas "shamanism" is an artificial category that is the result of colonialism, *noaidievhouta* is an indigenous and not a colonial name. By contrast, "Sámi shamanism ... [introduces] a theory-laden, generalising, and exoticizing concept to the already biased and one-sided textual sources we have to deal with."[11] The same remarks hold true of shamanism as it appears in the popular witchcraft books of the 1980s and '90s that I mentioned earlier. When Valiente, Cunningham and others invoke shamanism, they draw on a term with colonial baggage and contribute to the exoticized ideal of indigenous religions as seen by the interrogative Western gaze. As in the case of scholars of Sámi religion discussed by Kaikkonen, so too among contemporary witchcraft practitioners seeking to decolonize their discourse, it is really important to "discontinue" that gaze and everything it stands for.

However, discontinuing the Western gaze is not always straightforward. Kaikkonen reflects that replacing "Sámi shamanism" with *noaidevuohta* is complicated by the fact that a significant number of Sámi identifying as *noaidi* today nonetheless also describe themselves as shamans. During the 1980s and '90s Harner's *The Way of the Shaman* – and the tradition of Core Shamanism that Harner had begun to teach already in 1970s – became influential among indigenous practitioners reclaiming ancestral traditions in a global arena. Harner's influence was especially pronounced in Scandinavia, where early colonization (the Sámi were effectively Christianized by the end of the eighteenth century) has meant that there is now no living lineage of *noaidi* practising according to the old ways remembered in Sámi oral culture and documented in the accounts of missionaries and anthropologists. While there are still traditional healers and cunning folk among the Sámi,

11 Kaikkonen, "Some Observations and Suggestions," p10

their ritual framework today is Christian, and they no longer publicly employ the principal tool of the historical *noaidi*: the painted frame drum, an item that has since become iconic of the pre-Christian days of Sámi religion.

In the 1980s, Sámi practitioners wanting to revive the pre-Christian aspects of *noaidevuohta* often turned to Harner's work, and classes in Core Shamanism were taken by several soon-to-be influential figures in the revival of Sámi religion, among them Ailo Gaup (1944–2014). Gaup took classes in Core Shamanism and was the first self-declared Sámi "shaman" to make regular media appearances. Gaup was also controversial: adopted by a non-indigenous family, Gaup grew up in the south of Norway and only found his way back to the Sámi community as an adult. Nonetheless, his writings – poetry and novels as well as non-fiction – have been an important inspiration in the renaissance of Sámi religion.[12] Gaup used Harner's techniques but also drew from traditional Sámi healing as well as from historical accounts of the *noaidi* – in addition to learning from other indigenous practitioners the world over. When asked, in an interview, how much of his method was "authentically Sámi," Gaup explains:

> The starting point is Sámi: the local Sámi tradition of power animals, yoik (a traditional Sámi singing style also used by the noaidi) and the forces of nature; how the power travels through guides, power animals and ancestral spirits; understanding offerings, that we share energy. All of this I have received from the Sámi tradition. Later on I have moved from the local tradition to the global inheritance [of indigenous peoples] [...] If one is active in only one tradition it can become monotonous and require fresh nourishment and inspiration. I go where my inspiration takes me [...]

---

12 See for example, Gaup, Ailo, *In Search of the Drum*, trans. Bente Kjos Sjordal, Muse Publications,1993, and *The Night Between the Days*, trans. John Weinstock, Nordic Studies Press, 2010

I am in contact with several Amerindian shamans in South America and I experiment with their methods. But of course I remain active in a Sámi tradition.[13]

For Kaikkonen, the significance of shamanism in the work of Gaup and Gaup's students makes wholesale dismissal of the phrase "Sámi shamanism" impossible, at least where decolonization is concerned. In fact, Kaikkonen argues that, in the context of indigenous religion at least, shamanism needs to be more, not less, celebrated. Calling Gaup's form of Sámi religion "neo-shamanism," as some scholars have proposed in recent years, implies a pejorative Western perspective that does not do justice to the creative work undertaken by Gaup. At the same time, Kaikkonen insists that scholars (especially non-indigenous scholars) cannot continue to use "Sámi shamanism" to refer to the historical phenomenon of *noaidevuohta*. Sámi shamanism exists, and it is indeed indigenous – but only when it is voiced and reclaimed by the Sámi themselves. In other words, if an indigenous practitioner chooses to identify as a shaman, it is not up to a non-indigenous scholar – nor to a non-indigenous practitioner – to call them out and declare their practice somehow invalid or inauthentic. In the contemporary indigenous context, "shaman" can mean all sorts of things that are not at all obvious to the "interrogative Western gaze" which assumes the word can have only one (Western, colonial) meaning. Cadena reports a similar phenomenon from their field work in the Andes of South America. Cadena was surprised to find

> *"... shamanism needs to be more, not less, celebrated."*

---

13 Eriksson, Jörgen, *Vandrare i två världar: Samisk shamanism*, bok 2, Umeå: h:ström, 2004, pp126–7, My translation

that many local practitioners of traditional magic had begun to use "shamanism" (*chamanismo*) but that the word had taken on a sense that was quite distinctive to the local region and its traditions. *Chamanismo Andino*, whatever the word's colonial roots, today is an indigenous practice and irreducible to Western assumptions about "shamanism."[14]

What does this mean for witchcraft and the ethics of decolonization? Discontinuing colonial words is important. Equally important, though, is paying attention to the way colonial words have been reclaimed by indigenous communities as part of a movement to celebrate belonging in the face of centuries of violence and oppression. While the term "shamanism" is the product of colonialism and inseparable from a history of violence toward indigenous peoples, shamanism nonetheless now also has a history and usage of its own among indigenous practitioners reclaiming ancestral traditions. Recognizing that usage and allowing those who have created it to represent their practice freely, is now of the essence. As James Clifford writes in *Returns: Becoming Indigenous in the Twenty-First Century* (2013), indigeneity is complicated terrain. The worst enemy of decolonization is the conviction that there is only one use of a word – in our case, one sense of "shamanism" – that is valid or true. From the perspective of the scholar, decolonization does not take place in a state of suave assurance but in a state of "alert uncertainty." Clifford continues:

> no sovereign method is available, only experiments working outside the frozen alternatives of local and global, structure and process, macro and micro, material and cultural. We need to work at multiple scales and among discrepant histories, engaging with multiplicity and contradiction, inhabiting paradox.[15]

---

14 Cadena, *Earth Beings*, chapter 5
15 Clifford, James, *Returns: Becoming Indigenous in the Twenty-First Century*, Harvard University Press, pp45, 49

> *"These words, it seems to me, describe also what is at stake in the decolonization of modern witchcraft."*

For Clifford, decolonizing means not only unlearning the colonial but also learning with the indigenous in a post-colonial world. "Discrepant histories" are created whenever indigenous communities make colonial words their own, resisting colonial violence by transforming weapons of generalization into tools for individuation. Clifford calls this process "realism," by which he means the "overlapping … histories that struggle for room to manoeuvre in a paradoxically systematic and chaotic contemporary world."[16]

These words, it seems to me, describe also what is at stake in the decolonization of modern witchcraft. Too often when decolonization is mentioned by non-indigenous practitioners the discourse drifts towards a kind of idealism. Practitioners who, like myself, do not identify with an indigenous culture are likely to respond enthusiastically to the promise of a neutral language free of colonial baggage, forgetting that it is less the words themselves that make a difference and more the identity of the speaker. If the only voices debating "shamanism" are non-indigenous, how successful is the debate in terms of decentring Western terminology? Ultimately, decolonization is about communicating across cultures in a world of many practices.

---

16 Clifford, *Returns*, p49

SUGGESTED FURTHER READING

Cadena, Marisol de la, *Earth Beings: Ecologies of Practice Across Andean Worlds*, Duke University Press, 2015

Clifford, James, *Returns: Becoming Indigenous in the Twenty-First Century*, Harvard University Press, 2013

Eliade, Mircea, *Shamanism: Archaic Techniques of Ecstasy*, trans. W. Trask, Bollingen, 1964

Flaherty, Gloria, *Shamanism and the Eighteenth Century*, Princeton University Press, 1992

Gottlieb, Kathryn, "Cultural Appropriation in Contemporary Neopaganism and Witchcraft." MA dissertation. Honors College, 2017, https://digitalcommons. library.umaine.edu/honors/304

Harner, Michael, *The Way of the Shaman: A Guide to Power and Healing*, HarperCollins, 1980

Hutton, Ronald, *Shamans: Siberian Spirituality and the Western Imagination*, Continuum, 2001

Kaikkonen, Konsta, "Sámi indigenous(?) Religion(s)(?)— Some Observations and Suggestions Concerning Term Use," *Religions*, 2020, 11, 432, pp9-22

Lupa (ed.), *Talking About the Elephant: An Anthology of Neopagan Perspectives on Cultural Appropriation*, Megalithica, 2008

Nadeau, Denise, *Unsettling Spirit: A Journey into Decolonisation*, Queen's University Press, 2020

Rose, Deborah Bird, *Reports from a Wild Country: Ethics for Decolonisation*, University of New South Wales Press, 2004

Shamanic Arawak Priestess, YouTube channel, www.youtube.com/channel/ UCsgTZqGrRx-BSYKy0CKSjPg

Wallis, Robert J, *Shamans/Neo-Shamans: Ecstasy, Alternative Archaeology and Contemporary Pagans*, Routledge, 2003

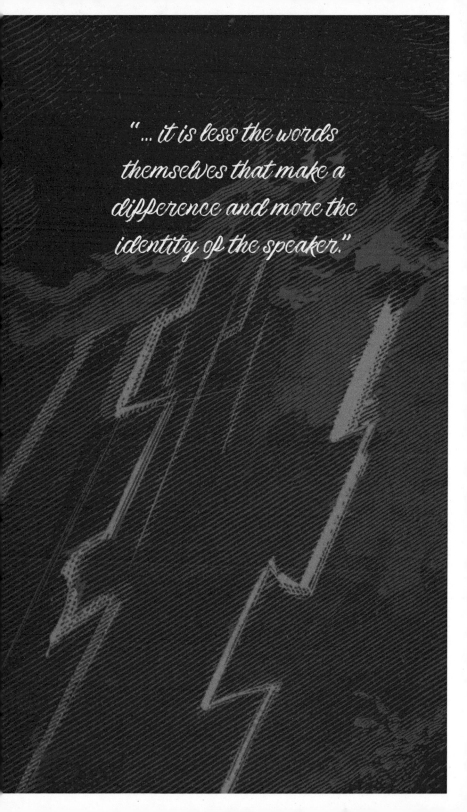

"... it is less the words themselves that make a difference and more the identity of the speaker."

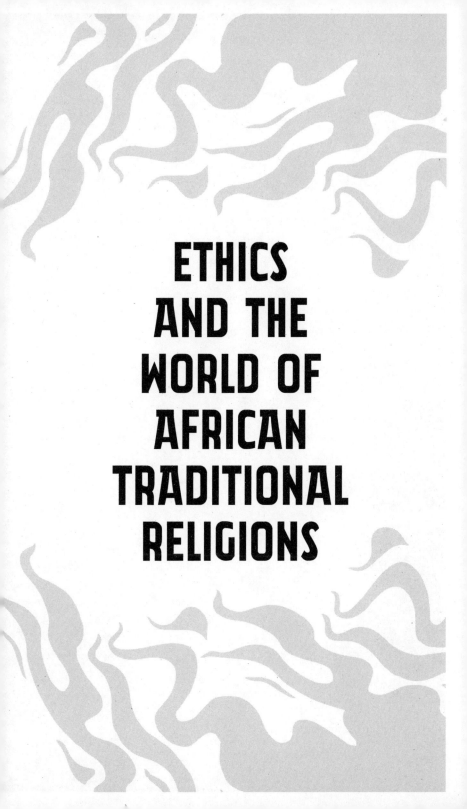

ETHICS
AND THE
WORLD OF
AFRICAN
TRADITIONAL
RELIGIONS

"*Over the years I've had thousands of questions about animal sacrifice, voodoo dolls and other stereotypical media misrepresentations.*"

9

ETHICS AND THE WORLD OF AFRICAN TRADITIONAL RELIGIONS

BY LILITH DORSEY

As a scholar and practitioner of these topics it is abundantly clear to me that the world of African Traditional Religions is one of the most maligned and misunderstood on the planet. This is particularly true when we come to speak on the difficult issue of ethics. The media and the annals of public opinion have presented a picture of New Orleans Voodoo, Haitian Vodou, La Regla Lucumi (Santeria), Candomble and the rest that glorifies the negative in favour of the extreme. The reality of the practices is much more nuanced and complex, especially when it comes to topics like animal sacrifice, spells, initiation and at the core of all of these ethics and ethical conduct. I have spent over three decades of my life studying the religion, both through education and initiation. Over the years I've had thousands of questions about animal sacrifice, voodoo dolls and other stereotypical media misrepresentations. In this piece I will attempt to begin to sort the actual facts from the accepted fiction.

When speaking of ethics and the ATRs (African Traditional Religions) most people's minds turn quickly to the question of animal sacrifice. The original roots of the word "sacrifice" lie

in the process of making something sacred[1]. In many of
these religions sacrifice is employed to feed the Loa or
Orisha both spiritually and physically. Loa and Orisha are
spiritual beings, from Haitian Vodou and La Regla Lucumì
respectively; it is a bit reductionist to think of them as
Gods and Goddesses, as many in the religion still consider
themselves monotheists. It is common practice for animal
sacrifice to be employed in the rituals for the Loa and
Orisha. The act of offering an animal up to the Divine is a
complicated process and one that is not carried out lightly.
In many spiritual houses much training and initiation is
required before someone is allowed to carry out this process.
Some groups have age or gender requirements, and all insist
the ceremonies be undertaken by highly trained practitioners.
Many have told me they only utilize these methods in serious
situations where they would be willing to give their own life
if necessary. This could be the healing of a partner or a child,
where a sacrifice is required to save their life, either because
of health reasons or extreme danger. Unfortunately many
of these individuals prefer to remain anonymous due to the
prejudice and ignorance that still plagues the religions.

Another issue that rarely comes to light on this controversial
topic is that when domestic animals are sacrificed in ceremony,
very often they are cooked and eaten by the community, or
otherwise donated to the poor and hungry. Instead of being
wasteful as many outside the religions assume, the sacrifices
have a multi-layered functionality and are seen as vitally
important to ensure the health and success of practitioners
and society as a whole. It is believed that the animal gives
their life so that the entire group can survive.

The number of people who want to discuss this while
wearing leather shoes or eating a burger made of animal flesh
is astonishing. The reality is animal sacrifices in the ATRs
are carried out much more efficiently than in the agricultural

---

1   Hedley, D, *Sacrifice, Transcendence and 'Making Sacred'*, Royal Institute of
Philosophy Supplement, 2011, 68, 257-268

industry. If most people were aware of what goes on in slaughterhouses they would have a rude awakening. There are a few spiritual houses in these traditions where sacrifice is not carried out on a regular basis and my own, the House of Maman Brigitte, is one of them. The House of Maman Brigitte is a New Orleans-based house dedicated to honouring the ancestors and the spiritual foremothers and forefathers of the Crescent City. Even though we do not offer animals in ritual, we do still see the value in that practice. We also see that the way people respond to instances of animal sacrifice for religious reasons often seem to be confined only to African-based religions and not those from other cultures who also practice animal sacrifice. Nor are they as rigorously applied to other instances in the general population where animals are killed for food or clothing. What are the real motivations behind these questions about animal sacrifice? Is it possible they are rooted in racism or socio-economic privilege?

Another misconception that comes to mind when talking about New Orleans Voodoo, Haitian Vodou and the rest when it comes to ethics is in the area of spells and workings. I've heard people expound that spells of any kind are dangerous, manipulative, unethical and downright wrong. Unfortunately Hollywood and the mainstream media have painted a different and demonized picture. The African Traditional Religions and witchcraft as a whole has been cast through a lens of evil and manipulation. We can see this in popular films like *Serpent and the Rainbow*, *Angel Heart* and even *Child's Play*. I talk about these in great detail in my book *Voodoo and African Traditional Religion*. In actual practice unfortunately there are sometimes negative individuals, which could be said of any religion. People will go to extreme lengths sometimes to get what they want, no matter what. But is this part of the African Traditional Religions? Are they inherently focused on negativity and manipulation? The short answer is no, the long answer is that the problem is complex. While the origins of the traditions in West Africa have been in place over 2,400 years, in more recent times the horrors of slavery have crafted a system that allows for protection and justice when the bulk of society does not. Over 400 years of slavery filled with kidnapping, murder, rape and every torture imaginable meant that the magick and religion of these people had to be strong to survive. Curses, hexes, spells and more were crafted where individuals had no other recourse, and that knowledge persisted, just as unfortunately the need for them has persisted too. Many of these individuals had no other choice but to protect themselves by any means necessary to ensure their survival.

Modern witchcraft also has its own interesting concepts regarding ethics. Very often you can hear dictates like "harm none" among these witches, which stems from the Wiccan Rede. On several occasions this has been explained to me to mean that their spellwork and magic are sent into the universe with the directive that it harm none. I'm sure this will definitely be seen as an unpopular opinion but I'm not convinced this type of instruction is possible, and definitely sure it doesn't reflect the history of either witchcraft or African Traditional Religion[2]. Magic to punish those who have wronged you is thousands of years old. The earliest known curse tablets, which were inscribed to cause harm using supernatural tactics, are known to date back to the fifth century BCE. Pacifism in the face of aggression could be seen as a noble tactic but it is ultimately a risky one.

> "Modern witchcraft also has its own interesting concepts regarding ethics."

---

2 McDonald, K, *Curse tablets. In Oscan in Southern Italy and Sicily: Evaluating Language Contact in a Fragmentary Corpus,* Cambridge Classical Studies, Cambridge University Press, 2015, pp133–166

The directive to "harm none" has always left a bad taste of privilege in my mouth, seeming like it is spoken by those who haven't been seriously harmed. When looking at the religions of people who were burned, tortured and abused for centuries, protection magic can stand in direct opposition to the words "harm none". In many ways these are difficult words, but they are in response to difficult situations, and generations upon generations of trauma. In this context being ethical can be viewed in a whole new light.

Looking at the history of the religion, it appears that many misconceptions have tainted public opinion for 500 years. Within the communities these practices originate from, none of these things are seen as unusual, but instead described as traditional. I cannot talk about ethics in this context without speaking about "good character," or *iwa pele* as it is referred to in the ATRs. This concept comes from West Africa where the basis for these religions lie. Good character in this context is roughly defined as knowing your place in society and in the universe and acting accordingly to improve the lives of all concerned. At its core iwa pele tells us that your ethical behaviour and your destiny are linked. Those who do not perform as their best, highest selves, will not succeed. Everyone has their own unique destiny and ethics are defined within that structure. Guided through both readings and rituals, followers can craft their best life.

Because of the secretive history of Voodoo and the African Traditional Religions, these questions of ethical spellcraft and sacrifice are, I suppose, somewhat understandable. The thing that is really puzzling however, is that no one is examining the real issue. What people need to be discussing in regards to the ATRs and witchcraft as a whole is common courtesy and respect. The most unethical stories in the community stem from violations of these tenets.

Initiation in the African Traditional Religions is one of the most important things that occurs. There are many different initiations that an individual will undergo in their lifetime, and they guarantee the success of the practitioner and the community as a whole. These ceremonies take place in the context of a godparent and godchild relationship. It is a system of spiritual checks and balances to make sure everything is done respectfully and properly. Devotees must be part of these communities, for there is no provision for self-initiation and solitary practice. There are many rules that must be followed during the process of initiation. Many of these rules have an ethical basis that runs deep. There are sexual taboos, dietary restrictions, and honour and respect for the elders is visibly demonstrated by participants at every turn. The ATRs are some of the most ethical systems that I have ever seen. Where it goes awry, which is the same with every religious system or hierarchy, is when specific people abuse their power. It may have been Lord Acton who originally said "Power tends to corrupt and absolute power corrupts absolutely," but this has been true for humans since their very beginnings. There is nothing in New Orleans Voodoo, Haitian Vodou or the other African Traditional Religions that is inherently unethical or immoral. There are unfortunately individuals who make selfish and damaging choices that taint the practices as a whole. One of my spiritual teachers likes to remind me that "The public loves to drag Voodoo down to its lowest common denominator." By that she means that the nightly news or the corner gossip will always spread the story about a practitioner who shot her partner, or dug up something, or someone they shouldn't have. Very rarely do they take the time and effort to see the reality of the practices, many of which are focused on community service and uplifting members at every opportunity. As recent times have seen, the African Traditional Religions gaining more journalistic attention and public acceptance[3], hopefully the misconceptions surrounding ethics will finally begin to disappear.

---

3   "Voodoo Is Part of Us" www.nytimes.com/2019/11/21/nyregion/fetgede-voodoo-haiti.html

" *Everyone has their own unique destiny and ethics are defined within that structure.*"

WITCHCRAFT
IN THE
ANTHROPOCENE

"The term 'seven year witch', coined by critic Peg Aloi, situates broader cultural interest in witchraft as a tidal force, which peaks once in around seven years, then disappears."

10

WITCHCRAFT IN THE ANTHROPOCENE

BY ALICE TARBUCK

*W*itchcraft in 2021 is a considerable industry. The term "seven year witch", coined by critic Peg Aloi, situates broader cultural interest in witchcraft as a force which peaks once in around seven years, then disappears. However, after the financial crash of 2008, and in the context of our increasingly digital lives, witchcraft has found a hungrier audience, broader dissemination and far more potential to become a profitable industry than ever before.

Whether or not religious or spiritual practices ought to operate on a for-profit basis is a conversation far broader and more wide-ranging than can be contained within this book. However, what can be said is that throughout all major world religions and spiritual practices, whether or not there is a cost-to-entry in terms of practice, there is usually a burgeoning industry that grows around accoutrements, accessories and tools. Once, in a shop in the Vatican, I heard a nun negotiate for a "bigger, no, bigger than that!" statue of the Virgin Mary for her convent. She was delighted to be informed that the Blessed Virgin, in this emanation, also glowed in the dark.

I, certainly, am not offering a blanket critique of occult shops, practitioners offering services or companies that sell products to promote a "witchcraft aesthetic" – after all, we live under late capitalism, and this is how popularity and success are measured: in cold hard sales. What it is important to do, on the other hand, is to contextualize these industries. We live in an unprecedented global ecological crisis – one that is only worsening, growing more pervasive, and altering irrevocably how we live.

Within the context of this climate destruction, contemporary witchcraft practice is divided: the work itself is often deeply connected to, and seeks to serve, steward and understand our earth, to advocate for its protection. However, contemporary witchcraft as an industry seeks to sell to consumers a vision of natural beauty, abundance and verdancy; a rhetoric concerned with "tuning in" to the world, and promising that the "tuning-in" will yield personal gain – growth, riches, beauty, delight. The world – and the universe beyond it – become objects interacted with in service of individual growth. What is more, communing with nature is portrayed as an individualistic pursuit, and one which requires equipment from that world – white sage/palo santo; crystals; wooden, glass and metal bowls; incense; fancy candles; rare and exotic herbs. We can even purchase hairstyles, clothing and special dress that seem to promise to turn us into "more of a witch".

> *"How might we find a genuine connection with the world in a time such as this?"*

This disjunct speaks to a broader alienation between the self, considered as an individual, and the world, considered as other. Such dualism is, of course, the preserve of Enlightenment thinking and well-documented. But it is important to consider what might happen if that alienation was put down. If the claims of the witchcraft industry are to be listened to, if we are to surround ourselves with crystals and really "tune-in", "connect" and "ascend to higher planes", then what might await us, there? How might we find a genuine connection with the world in a time such as this?

It is almost certainly the case that the planet is suffering. That its systems are breaking down, under the vast economic and industrial burden we place upon it. When we slip a crystal into our pocket to "promote health" or "increase good vibrations", what are we actually inviting into our lives? Crystals are easy to buy, largely inexpensive and immediately accessible. Moreover, they always come glittering with promises, guarantees of their qualities – and there are hundreds of books and articles that detail how to use them for maximum benefit.

But, as journalist Tess McClure wrote in the *Guardian* in 2019, "demand for 'healing' crystals is soaring – but many are mined in deadly conditions in one of the world's poorest countries".[1] Much has been written about blood diamonds or conflict diamonds – gems mined in appalling conditions, often to fund wars, dubious military operations and to provide income to tyrannical regimes.[2] As a result of high-profile and widespread campaigns, many consumers of the precious stones now opt for lab-grown diamonds or diamonds that come with a guarantee of their ethical origin. Moreover, the diamond industry – and the precious gem industry more broadly – has been forced to alter its practices, and become more transparent about the origins and ethics of its products.

The multi-million pound global crystals industry, however, has not. Although not considered precious gems, crystals are still also rare and precious, and are similarly mined from the ground. Their geographic distribution means that many deposits of particular crystals exist in developing countries with exploitative labour practices; or in dangerous, difficult-to-access places; or embedded within protected land, delicate ecosystems, or places best left undisturbed. All mining is damaging to the ecology of the area it takes place in, to a greater or lesser extent. Contemporary witchcraft's apparent modalities of healing can, therefore, be means of ecological

---

1   "Dark crystals: the brutal reality behind a booming wellness craze", Health & wellbeing, *The Guardian,* www.theguardian.com
2   Conflict diamonds, Blood diamonds, *Global Witness,* www.globalwitness.org

destruction. It is important for us to consider how we use crystals, how we source them and who it is that we impact when we do. If the Wiccan Rede "And it harm none/do what thou wilt" is to be followed, then we must think of who our magic might harm, far beyond spells and curses – those who might have suffered to make our magic possible. And that includes the earth.

However, both magic and the environment can be united in a common solution. Everywhere one goes, there are rocks, pebbles, grit. Some are more precious and sacred than others. For example, there are rocks in Hawaii believed to be sacred to Pele. Tourists removed these, thinking that the rocks might bring them luck, and then learned that in fact, a curse would follow anyone who stole them. When this became more common knowledge, tourists began to post them back, asking for them to be returned to the beach.[3] However, in the main, rocks above ground can be, in small quantities, taken away. These loose stones are just as ancient as crystals mined from the ground. They are similarly charged by the deep magic of the earth, and by cycles and cycles of the moon. "Pebbles not crystals!" seems an ecological solution, and a rallying cry against unethical mining practices. There are two impediments to simply replacing one's crystal collection with beach pebbles, though, which can give pause. The first is that their individual magical aspects can be difficult to classify. Crystals and gems often have very particular uses and qualities, and these are enumerated clearly in books. Pebbles, however, are not so straightforward to interpret, and not everyone wishes to turn amateur geologist. This is not, however, insurmountable. Usually, small rocks and pebbles are easily identified as belonging to the dominant rock of the surrounding area – a quick internet search can solve that. Beyond this, it is important to understand that meaning is almost never innate,

---

3   This curse is erroneous, but nevertheless, many believe it. "Hawaii's hot rocks blamed by tourists for bad luck; Goddess said to curse those who take a piece of her island", www.sfgate.com

but rather ascribed. Qualities can be identified, but someone must do it. If a pebble is particularly ancient, it may be useful for steadiness. If it is shaped like an organ of the body – as is the case for magical healing stones in Highland Perthshire – then it may be useful for healing.[4]

Often, we come across rocks and pebbles at significant times or in significant company – these may be used to promote the mood or reflect the events around you at the time of finding. I have many river-pebbles from lucky days, hard days, days when I was ill, days when I was healing. These, I label, and use in magic as one would crystals. Additionally, their qualities may be clear – stones containing quartz, mica or iron, for example, are often found washed up on beaches – the crystal or element need not be the entirety of the object for it to be potent. There are also strategies of simply sitting and waiting for the pebble to let you know its best use. This is a lovely, meditative practice, which allows you to form a relationship with the rock. These strategies all reduce our reliance on crystals and, indeed, deepen our relationships to the world that surrounds us.

The second reason that the possibilities of the pebble remain underexplored is their aesthetic. Listen. There is no convincing argument that I can give you here, except that witchcraft aesthetics, as they are figured by the late capitalist internet, have nothing to do with the power or success of actual magic. Historically, practitioners of the occult have always prized the rare, the strange, the beautiful – we are no different. Where we diverge, however, is in understanding the larger cost of these objects. If we can lean into hedge-witchery, kitchen-witchery, which both make-do with what is around, which practise magic of the between-places, the domestic spaces, the overlooked ground, then perhaps we can also embrace an "eco-witchery", which reduces, re-uses, recycles and draws power precisely from knowing that it is in support of our great planet. At the very least, if witchcraft is an expression of our

---

4   See this article on St Fillan's Healing Stones: "Healing Stones of Saint Fillan – Nessie's Grotto", *Lochness Monster*, simegen.com

will into the world, we might be satisfied that our will is not to harm.

Crystals, in all their glittering temptation, are only the tip of the iceberg. Modern witchcraft draws on diverse religious and spiritual practices, often appropriating closed practices lifted from indigenous peoples or selling imitations of objects sacred to certain folk practices. Dream catchers, for example, which originate with the Cree people, are often sold in spiritual shops, and there is heated debate over whether or not their creation and sale by non-native peoples is appropriation. One commenter noted that it was the volume and mass-production of them that was offensive. "It has gotten out of hand. It's disrespectful for our people. It means something to us, it's a tradition," said Benjamin, a member of the Mille Lacs Band of Ojibwe.[5] While some objects and practices are grey areas, it is nevertheless important to understand that others are not – especially when it comes to ecological crisis. Palo Santo, a plant which is also known as white sage, is an example of an ingredient sacred to folk tradition that has been exploited by Western occultism almost to the point of extinction. The plant is a woody bush – its Latin name is *bursera graveolens* – and it grows in Mexico, Guatemala, Honduras, taking 50–70 years to reach maturity. Even once it is mature and harvested, it takes a while for the oils within it to develop prior to use. Like many holy substances, Palo Santo was historically comparatively rare, hard to come by and to be used sparingly. Traditionally, this wasn't a problem, but as the practice of

> *"Crystals, in all their glittering temptation, are only the tip of the iceberg."*

---

5   Dream Catcher (cultural appropriation), *Native News Network*, https://nativenewsnetwork.posthaven.com

smoke cleansing (which is sometimes called smudging) grew in popularity around the world, the plant became scarcer, and its habitat, which is under threat from industrialization more generally, has decreased.

The difficulties with Palo Santo are, however, not simply ecological. They are also cultural. Quoted in the New York Times, Chelsey Luger, who works with Well for Culture, an indigenous wellbeing initiative, commented that the atmospheric Instagram photographs of people using Palo Santo to smudge, out its original context, were actively erasing indigenous people from narratives around spirituality and magic: "They're using our culture but removing our faces from the picture. It forwards the narrative that we don't exist and that we're not experts in our own fields and heritage", she says.[6] And this erasure is deeply pernicious. It sends the message that we can simply cherry-pick whatever appeals to us, without reference to its originators. It is appropriative cultural plagiarism, which places aesthetics over functionality, and what attracts social media attention over what is effective, appropriate magical practice.

What is even more difficult about contemporary witchcraft's misplaced obsession with Palo Santo is that humans have been using smoke to disinfect and clean their dwellings throughout history, especially in colder countries. Smudging relates only to a small number of indigenous practices – smoke cleansing itself is not only an open practice, it is also a far-reaching and varied one. Scotland, for example, has a rich smoke cleansing tradition, known as "redding", or "saining".[7] This tradition grew out of functional smoke cleansing. The principle is exactly the same – plants with cleansing properties, for example, rosemary, juniper, some types of fir, are burned in a confined space until the space is packed with smoke, and then the smoke

6   "Is Palo Santo Endangered?", *The New York Times*, www.nytimes.com
7   https://cailleachs-herbarium.com/2019/02/saining-not-smudging-purification-and-lustration-in-scottish-folk-magic-practice/

is slowly allowed to evaporate outward. The smoke from these plants contains antimicrobial and anti-viral properties, and can help to destroy lingering illness or stale air, of the sort that would build up over winter in poorly ventilated, damp accommodation. Saining, however, as Scott Richardson-Read writes, "were carried out primarily to remove influences of negative spirits on people, places, objects and livestock" – a ritualized version of this cleansing.[8] Blessing or cleansing a space with smoke is also a feature of Christianity – the censer processing down through a church sends sweet scent heavenward and cleanses the interior of the holy space. Smoke – and indeed, fire – have always been foundational to spiritual practice, as has the burning of specifically medicinal and aromatic plants to release their oils. The fact that smudging became de rigeur among contemporary magic practitioners is perhaps unsurprising, but it is telling that interest in smoke cleansing did not extend to encompass Western folk practices. What we can do to repair these harms is to consider, when we encounter a closed practice, or even a practice belonging to colonized people, whether it is necessary that we learn it or practise it. Whether or not we have the skills and contextual knowledge to do so? What we think we would get from the practice and whether there might be something already extant in our own folk histories that might answer that need instead. Rather than reaching our hands out, and expecting them to be filled, it would benefit us to become curious about our own witchcraft and folk magic histories.

Witchcraft, if it is to be relevant to us in the present moment, in late capitalism, in ecological crisis, must be capable of stepping outside the received systems of production and consumption. It must be capable of questioning the current world order, of collecting what is discarded, what is overlooked, and bringing it into relation. Bringing it into the light. We are sold an idea of witchcraft as being something

---

8   Ibid

that takes place slightly outside our present cultural moment. It is conducted, many books would have us believe, most successfully in virgin forests, on high mountains, at well-heads and in remote deserts. This picture of "untouched" wilderness as the most receptive and potent place for our magic is, of course, an impossibility – another vision that we are sold in the hope we might purchase objects or experiences that attempt to recreate and capture it. These places are largely impossible and imaginary – we are all, now, touched by the Anthropocene trace of our interference with the planet's systems – from microplastics in our organs to trace metals in the food we eat. Landscapes, however remote, are the same. It is incumbent on us to work instead with what we have – with pebbles, and half-burnt candles. With robes made from old dressing gowns, and offering vessels that double as egg-cups. There is nothing wrong with beauty, but we must be wary of its

> "Magic happens in our imperfect bodies, and in our imperfect landscapes."

apparent virtue – we must, instead, investigate its costs. Why would we do better magic after spending six hours climbing a mountain than we would in our cosy living rooms, with our favourite music on, gazing down at the pavement beneath us or at cars speeding along the motorway. Magic happens in our imperfect bodies, and in our imperfect landscapes. We cannot gain the world's trust, help it, help ourselves, until we accept that everything is linked – from trees to trash cans, crystals to pebbles, human exploitation on one side of the world to bad magic on the other.

There's no one way to do magic, of course – and that is half the problem with witchcraft. It doesn't have a right or wrong, really, and so much of the advice comes from people who want power, people who want to sell you something, charismatic individuals whose methods are adopted by a sufficiently significant group of people. So many of the commonly incorporated rituals that are taken for granted in contemporary witchcraft have their origins in strange perversions of closed ritual practices, or the adoption of certain desirable objects with no clear origins in actual magical writing. So much of our magic in the current moment focuses on performing to a camera, acquiring objects, acquiring "likes". Ritual and theatre have their place, but I have a preference for inclusive magic, for magic that is written with acknowledgement of time constraints; of complex, messy human lives. Magic that seeks to hold our planet, not exploit it. Magic that resists consumption and instead tries to pour our gifts onto the world – gifts of care, gifts of time, gifts of attention. That is the sort of magic that draws me and which I can practically execute. Magic that feeds and heals and helps is open to us all. We can do it wherever we are, with whatever we have to hand. Slip your fingers into your pocket – you may already find a pebble there. And that is all you need to get started. The world is ready. Are you?

"Ritual and theatre have their place, but I have a preference for inclusive magic."

A NEW
MALLEUS
MALEFICARUM

"The term 'witch hunt' ... has become a favourite in recent times among those seeking to push an authoritarian agenda."

11

A NEW *MALLEUS MALEFICARUM*: THE MYTH OF THE GENDER- CRITICAL WITCH HUNT

BY CLAIRE ASKEW

*T*he term "witch hunt" wasn't widely used until Arthur Miller popularized it in his 1953 play *The Crucible*. Written as an allegory in response to McCarthyism, Miller claimed to have based the play on the true story of the 1692 Salem witch trial – an event that led to the execution of twenty people and the torture and imprisonment of dozens more. *The Crucible* is in fact a largely fabricated story, which sees Miller sexualize a child (the real Abigail Williams was eleven years old in 1692 – in *The Crucible* she is seventeen) and then place the blame for the entire "witch hunt" on her wanton promiscuity. While writing *The Crucible*, Miller was conducting an extra-marital affair with Marilyn Monroe, and his protagonist – a heavily fictionalized version of John Proctor, one of the six men executed at Salem in 1692 – is clearly something of a self-insert[i].

The term "witch hunt" – whose dictionary definition is "an attempt to find and punish people whose opinions are unpopular and who are said to be a danger to society"[ii] – has become a favourite in recent times among those seeking to push an authoritarian agenda. The term has become almost synonymous with Donald Trump, who used it regularly before becoming President of the United States[iii], and while in office, tweeted the term once every three days, on average[iv]. Trump's definition of "witch hunt" is apparently "any kind of scrutiny, however justified": the things he referred to as witch hunts included public interest in his tax returns; his mishandling of the USA's response to the COVID-19 pandemic; investigations into alleged criminal activity at the Trump Organisation; the Mueller investigation and his two articles of impeachment[v].

A variety of right-wing groups have subsequently adopted the term "witch hunt," no doubt following Trump's lead. Most notable is the co-option and frequent misuse of witch hunt rhetoric by the self-styled "gender-critical" movement: a mostly-online gathering of men and women who seek to limit the legal rights and freedoms of transgender, non-binary and other gender-nonconforming people. They call themselves "gender criticals" or "GCs," but they are also widely known as TERFs (a term they deem a slur, in spite of its accuracy: TERF stands for trans-exclusionary radical feminist).

The exclusion of queer, trans, non-binary and gender non-conforming folk is a serious problem in the witchcraft community. Hugely popular books on contemporary witchcraft define magic as something gender essentialist: as "pussy-power and our innate feminine wisdom," and "the power that lies between our thighs […] a womb-deep recognition."[vi] The author of this same book writes in its opening chapter, "I thought: I'll piss off the transgender community for not addressing them … yet this is the work I do. I do women's work, and I'm definitely not going to apologize for that." Note that "the transgender community" does not, in this author's eyes, include women. The book currently boasts 2,076 Amazon reviews and a 4.5 star average rating – the witches reading it don't seem to have a problem with its cheerful exclusion.

Even "witchcraft 101" style resources that don't knowingly exclude queer, trans, non-binary and gender non-conforming witches often fail to acknowledge that anything exists beyond the idea of gender as a binary. The witch is very often referred to as a general "she": "she's an intelligent, resilient being who changes with the times, and changes the times along with her. One thing is certain: a witch is almost always a *she*."[vii] Elsewhere, Erica Jong boldly states, "we *always* imagine the witch as female – and the Devil as male" (italics mine)[1]. All too often, contemporary witchcraft literature makes reference to the witch as having a specific, and gender essentialist, anatomy: Lisa Lister's talk of wombs and "pussy power," or, in one of Jong's poems, the moment where a witch's face is directly compared to female genitalia.[ix]

So, there are many so-called witches out there who are actively trans exclusionary, and still more who just don't seem to really consider or engage with queer, trans, non-binary or gender non-conforming folk. This is not only a problem because it narrows the scope of our occult communities and creates spaces that are inaccessible or even unsafe for minority witches. It's a problem because it feeds – deliberately or not – into revisionist ideas about witch hunts, and the thousands of people persecuted and killed in their name. It's a problem because it feeds into the growing problem of organized transphobia, and allows TERFs and other right-wing groups to co-opt witch hunt imagery as a way of justifying the very real harms that they do. (I have neither the space nor the strength to devote to an analysis of these harms, and I don't want to make this essay any more triggering than it already is. Happily, Judith Butler does a better job of summing up the gender-critical movement than I ever could, writing in the *Guardian*:

> As a fascist trend, the anti-gender movement supports ever strengthening forms of authoritarianism. Its tactics encourage

---

1   Bear in mind, these are not history books: the author is not talking about the so-called "witch" of old – actually a marginalized person who was persecuted – and usually executed – over fabricated witchcraft claims. Those people often were women, and I'll get to them later in this essay. These authors are referring to a contemporary, generally aspirational witch figure – a figure the reader is meant to be able to access and identify with.

state powers to intervene in university programs, to censor art and television programming, to forbid trans people their legal rights, to ban LGBTQI people from public spaces, to undermine reproductive freedom and the struggle against violence directed at women, children, and LGBTQI people. It threatens violence against those, including migrants, who have become cast as demonic forces and whose suppression or expulsion promises to restore a national order under duress.[x]

TERFs began using witch hunt rhetoric in earnest around 2017 – and indeed, they were particularly interested in *The Crucible* as a template from which to draw their ideas about witchcraft persecution. As Twitter commentator @judeinlondon2 noted in January 2018, "TERFs are changing their twitter names to "Goody [insert name here]" which is the most hilarious irony"[xi] – in *The Crucible*, female characters were referred to as "Goody", a polite form of address in 1692, and a shortening of "Goodwife." TERF accounts used "Goody" as a way to quickly identify one another as being part of the gender-critical movement[2], but they chose this prefix carefully. Using it was an attempt by gender-critical individuals to align themselves with the executed "witches" of Arthur Miller's play, and by extension, with persecuted witches in general. It was a handy, shorthand way of crying "witch hunt."

Why is this – as @judeinlondon2 puts it – hilariously ironic? In order to understand, we need to look not at the fictionalized witch hunts of *The Crucible*, but at the very real witchcraft trials that Miller, Trump and the so-called gender criticals are referencing. Starting in the mid-1500s, a wave of witchcraft paranoia – sometimes called the witch craze or witchcraft hysteria – swept much of the northern hemisphere, and stuck around for two full centuries. During this time,

---

2   Some also included the suffix "XX" in their Twitter handle or description, a reference to XX chromosomes, which TERFs mistakenly believe to be "female" chromosomes. In truth, though many women do have XX chromosomes, not all do: sex determination by chromosome is far more nuanced than this.

witchcraft trials sprang up across Europe and Scandinavia, with the fringes of this paranoia also reaching the fairly new North American colonies. Countries particularly affected included Germany, France, Sweden, England and Scotland. Henry VIII passed the first official Witchcraft Act in the British Isles in 1542, and the Act was extended by Elizabeth I in 1563, which was also the year that the Scottish Witchcraft Act was passed. Between 1550 and 1650, an estimated 4,000 "witches" were executed in the British Isles[xii]: that's almost one per week. Though numbers vary from country to country, it's estimated that around 85 per cent of accused witches were female[xiii]. In Scotland, that number rises to 90 per cent[xiv].

"85 per cent of accused witches were female."

What were these people being executed for, exactly?

In the case of Goodwife Glover (her first name was not preserved in the historical record), who was executed in Boston, Massachusetts in 1688, it was for being "an ignorant and a scandalous old woman in the neighbourhood, whose miserable husband before he died had sometimes complained of her that she was undoubtedly a witch."[xv] Glover was subject to a trial she didn't understand, and as a way of proving her innocence, she was asked to recite the Lord's Prayer in English. Though the court acknowledged that Glover spoke only Gaelic [referred to in court documents as "Irish"], and that "she owned herself a Roman Catholic and could recite her Pater Noster in Latin very readily,"[xvi] she was still sentenced to death.

In the case of Merga Bien – one of over 200 accused "witches" put to death in the German city of Fulda in the three years from 1603 to 1606[xvii] – it was for marrying a third man after two previous husbands died, but not falling pregnant until the fourteenth year of their marriage. Rather than being seen as a good reason for a stay of execution, Bien's pregnancy was considered an aggravating circumstance: the only explanation for such an "unnatural" event was, of course, intercourse with the Devil. Bien was burned at the stake.

In the case of many Scottish witches, a case was built around the supposed ability of the accused to radically change their appearance: "in order to transport themselves from one place to another [or] to enable them to enter people's houses without being recognized."[xviii] The most famous of these shape-shifting witches is Isobel Gowdie, tried in Auldearn in 1662. In a lengthy confession elicited under torture, Gowdie spoke of, "charms for changing ... into hares, cats or crows – and back again,"[xix] as well as "the secret of slipping away from the marital bed unnoticed" by enchanting a broom or stool:

> And lest our husbands should miss us owt of our beddis, we put in a besom, or a thrie-leggit stool besyde them, and then say thrice ower, I lay down this besom, or stool, and in the Devillis name, let it not stir ... while I come again. And immediatlie it seemis a woman beside our husbands.[xx]

There were many documents circulating during the roughly two centuries in question, which may have been drawn upon for instruction in the ways of finding and prosecuting witches. However, by far the most famous of these was the German volume *Malleus Maleficarum*, or "Hammer of Witches," written in 1486 by clergyman Heinrich Kramer (sometimes credited as Henricus Institor). Silvia Federici calls the *Malleus*, "possibly the most misogynous text ever written,"[xxi] while Kristen J Sollée points out that the book, "inspired countless cruel deaths, but was pretty much ye olde medieval BDSM erotica."[xxii] The *Malleus* was an early book on the identification of witches – it was also a popular one, and went into incredible depth about the characteristics and activities of the so-called witch. It influenced most of the witchcraft literature that came after it, and in turn, informed witchcraft legislation across Europe and in the early American colonies.

It is from the *Malleus* that we get the idea that a witch is likely to be a woman: the book's most-quoted line is, "all witchcraft comes from carnal lust, which is in women insatiable."[xxiii] But as well as taking a keen interest in women's sexuality – with whom they might be having sex, and how often – the *Malleus* is also deeply preoccupied with genitalia, and especially with the penis or "member." It warns that witches are generally interested in "obstructing [the] generative force ... removing the members accommodated to that act, [and] changing men into beasts."[xxiv] Penises may be literally severed, the book says, or otherwise made to disappear via "some prestidigitatory illusion so that the male organ *appears* to be entirely removed"[xxv] (italics mine). Kristen J Sollée notes: "there's also a fantastical description of witches stealing penises and keeping them as pets in a bird's nest."[xxvi]

In short, the public perception of witches at this time was extremely gendered, and ideas about sexuality and gender identity were deeply enmeshed with the image of the witch in the collective imagination. P G Maxwell-Stuart, in his comprehensive work *The British Witch: The Biography*, draws our attention to a popular play written in 1538 by "controversialist" clergyman John Bale, in which "the female witch's range of accomplishments"[xxvii] are personified as characters named, among other things, Idolatry, Faithlessness and (at this point, please imagine an "eyeballs" emoji) Sodomy. At one point in the play, Faithlessness asks Idolatry, "Were you at one time a man?", and Idolatry replies, "Yes, but now I am a woman." Maxwell-Stuart notes that:

> Idolatry would have been played by a man dressed as a woman. Thus, the notion that idolatry ... feminizes men and turns them into parodies of what men ought to be unmistakably suggests to the audience that a witch destroys the natural order of things and subverts God's laws.

He goes on to provide his own definition of a witch as:

> *A person in a community whose speech and behaviour*
> *that community judged, estimated, commented on, and*
> *sometimes complained about [...] Male magicians were*
> *likely to be seen as unnaturally feminized, and women as*
> *irrational, behaviourally uncontrolled individuals in need of*
> *boundaries, and needing to have those boundaries policed*
> *and enforced.*[xxviii]

I don't think I need to over-egg this particular pudding: it's clear to me that TERFs are absolutely correct to assert that – in their attitudes to and dealings with queer, trans, non-binary and gender non-conforming folk – they are indeed at the centre of a contemporary witch hunt. They're just using the term backwards. J K Rowling – who, on 22nd September 2020, tweeted a photograph of herself wearing a t-shirt that read "This Witch Doesn't Burn"[3] – may have encouraged many of her gender critical followers to put on the costume of the persecuted witch, but the idea that the TERFs are the victimized party is, frankly, laughable. It's a classic example of DARVO, which stands for deny, attack, reverse victim and offender.

The people who executed Goodwife Godwin did so because she was considered scandalous – because she was an outsider, who used language the people around her didn't understand. The people who executed Merga Bien did so because she didn't conform to traditional ideas about what marriage or child-rearing should look like. The people who executed Isobel Gowdie did so in fear of the idea that she might be able to change her appearance, to pass unnoticed through spaces where she wasn't wanted. The people who nodded along to John Bale's play wanted those who might be participating in sodomy to be

---

3   The t shirt originated from a shop named Wild Womyn Boutique, which also sells goods with slogans like "transactivism is misogyny" and "woman is not a costume."

executed, too. The people who read and circulated the *Malleus Maleficarum* were fixated by the image of the bewitched penis, disembodied and roaming around. These accusers fuelled an entire two-hundred-year witch craze by repeatedly stoking a fear of people who didn't conform to the stubbornly gendered norms of the period. Is it me, or do these people sound an awful lot like our contemporary "gender criticals"?

If anyone in the contemporary world has a right to cry witch hunt, then queer, trans, non-binary and gender non-conforming folk do. Trans people in the UK are twice as likely to be the victims of crime than cis people[xxix]. Between 1 October 2019 and 30 September 2020, 350 trans and gender-diverse people were murdered – a majority of the victims were black or people of colour, and many were sex workers[xxx]. The average waiting time to access a first appointment at a gender identity clinic in the UK was 18 months in 2020, with some people waiting up to three years for an initial consultation[xxxi]. All of this against a backdrop of "gender critical" lobbying designed to strip away queer, trans, non-binary and gender non-conforming individuals' rights to, among other things, "legal and institutional safeguards against gender discrimination, forced psychiatric internment, brutal physical harassment and killing."[xxxii]

I'll leave you with the words of trans witch J Inscoe, who writes:

> When I think of the religious persecution of folk based on accusation of the supernatural, I think about the particular ease with which the language of the witch fits the experiences of transgender, nonbinary, and other gender non-conforming individuals. [...] Because of the essentialist usage of "witch," the act of "burning the witch" becomes deeply linked with the recent outcries against a cancel culture. [...] But of course, any trans, nonbinary or gender non-conforming person can tell you that the "open debate" on our rights is more so open season. [xxxiii]

REFERENCES

i Dahvana Headley, Maria "Him Too? How Arthur Miller Smeared Marilyn Monroe and Invented the Myth of the Male Witch Hunt", *The Daily Beast*, 27 January 2018, www.thedailybeast.com/him-too-how-arthur-miller-smeared-marilyn-monroe-and-invented-the-myth-of-the-male-witch-hunt

ii *Cambridge Advanced Learner's Dictionary*, 4th Edition, Cambridge University Press, 2013

iii Markham-Cantor, Alice, "What Trump Really Means When He Cries 'Witch Hunt'", *The Nation*, 28 October 2019, www.thenation.com/article/archive/trump-witch-hunt/

iv Almond, Philip C "You think this is a witch hunt, Mr President? That's an insult to the women who suffered", *The Conversation*, 20 January 2020, https://theconversation.com/you-think-this-is-a-witch-hunt-mr-president-thats-an-insult-to-the-women-who-suffered-129775

v Frankel, Jeffrey, "The three most misused phrases in US politics in 2020". *The Guardian*, 29 December 2020, www.theguardian.com/business/2020/dec/29/us-politics-2020-witch-hunt-black-swan

vi Lister, Lisa, *Witch: Unleashed. Untamed. Unapologetic*, Hay House, 2017

vii Kitaiskaia, Taisia, *Literary Witches: A Celebration of Magical Women Writers*, Seal Press, 2017

viii Jong, Erica, *Witches*, Harry N Abrams Inc, 2004

ix Ibid

x Butler, Judith, "Why is the idea of 'gender' provoking backlash the world over?", *The Guardian*, 23 October 2021, www.theguardian.com/us-news/commentisfree/2021/oct/23/judith-butler-gender-ideology-backlash

xi Judeinlondon2 tweeted this on Jan 28th 2018

xii Schiff, Stacy, *The Witches: Salem 1692, A History*, Little Brown, 2015

xiii Ehrenreich, Barbara and Deirdre English, *Witches, Midwives & Nurses: A History of Women Healers*, The Feminist Press, 2010

xiv Seafield, Lily, *Scottish Witches*, Waverley Books, 2009

xv Howe, Katherine, "Goodwife Glover, Boston, Massachusetts, 1688" *The Penguin Book of Witches*, Penguin, 2014

xvi Ibid

xvii Mastin, Luke "The Witch Trials: Fulda Witch Trials 1603–1606", *Witchcraft: A Guide to the Misunderstood and Maligned*, 2009, http://www.lukemastin.com/witchcraft/trials_fulda.html

xviii Seafield, Lily, *Scottish Witches*, Waverley Books, 2009

xix Ibid

xx Ibid

xxi Federici, Silvia, *Witches, Witch-Hunting and Women*, PM Press, 2018

xxii Sollée, Kristen J, *Witches Sluts Feminists: Conjuring the Sex Positive*, Stone Bridge Press, 2017

xxiii Karlsen, Carol F, *The Devil in the Shape of a Woman: Witchcraft in Colonial New England*, Vintage, 1989

xxiv Ibid

xxv Sollée, Kristen J, *Witches Sluts Feminists: Conjuring the Sex Positive*, Stone Bridge Press, 2017

xxvi Ibid

xxvii Maxwell-Stuart, P G, *The British Witch: The Biography*, Amberley, 2014

xxviii Ibid

xxix Walker, Amy, "Trans people twice as likely to be victims of crime in England and Wales" *The Guardian*, 17 July 2020, www.theguardian.com/society/2020/jul/17/trans-people-twice-as-likely-to-be-victims-of-in-england-and-wales

xxx "TMM Update: Trans Day of Remembrance 2020" *Transrespect Versus Transphobia*, 11 November 2020, https://transrespect.org/en/tmm-update-tdor-2020/

xxxi "Transgender people face NHS waiting list 'hell'" *BBC News*, 9 January 2020, www.bbc.co.uk/news/uk-england-51006264

xxxii Butler, Judith, "Why is the idea of 'gender' provoking backlash the world over?", *The Guardian*, 23 October 2021 www.theguardian.com/us-news/commentisfree/2021/oct/23/judith-butler-gender-ideology-backlash

xxxiii Inscoe, J "Trans/figuring the witch: On J K Rowling and the TERF mystique" *Linguistic Society of America*, 2020, www.linguisticsociety.org/content/transfiguring-witch-jk-rowling-and-terf-mystique

"If anyone in the contemporary world has a right to cry witch hunt, then queer, trans, non-binary and gender non-conforming folk do."

"WHAT ARE YOU FIGHTING?"

"*I was scared.
I asked the tarot and,
at first glance, the answer
was not what I expected ...*"

12

"WHAT ARE YOU FIGHTING?" GENDER, WITCHCRAFT AND THE HIGH PRIESTESS FROM ONE NONBINARY WITCH'S PERSPECTIVE

BY EM STILL

Content note: *This article makes mention of some things that could be triggering, including gender dysphoria, violence against trans people (alluded not explicit), addiction, depression and suicide.*

Yule 2019: I was angry, uncomfortable, and addicted. For my whole life I had been faking, and in the spirit of Yule I wanted to leave that behind. Desperate for joy, it was time to face everything.

I knew I was trans, somewhere. I had said as much out loud once or twice. But, I fought and denied. I was scared. I asked the tarot and, at first glance, the answer was not what I expected.

OUR PRIESTESS SITS ON A COLD STONE

The High Priestess at first glance is a card of femininity and balance, the dichotomy of the palm trees and pomegranates as well as the body symbolism of the two pillars versus the opening of the temple and water behind her, make this card one of the most gendered in the deck. And, yet this card acknowledges power structures of religion, of gender roles and the magic in breaking them.

The play of gender, power, symbolism and magic interests me as a nonbinary person. What do all these vast cultures, religions, and powers mean to a trans witch living today?

EITHER/OR, NEITHER/OR

I am nonbinary. I use they/them pronouns and do not use gendered language in reference to myself. Nonbinary is a category – a heading. While not every genderqueer person wants to be referred to as such[1] it has entered the mainstream as a kind of "third"[2] option to our traditionally two-way system.

WHAT ARE YOU FIGHTING?

When I sat with the cards, I faced what I had spent as long as I could remember fearing. I asked what I was fighting. I asked about gender. The cards gave me the High Priestess.

What struck me was the inbetween, the way she is centred on the card looking directly out. She is a master of this space. I was struck by how comfortable she looked surrounded by the trappings of religion and symbols of the body.

I have been devoted to the High Priestess ever since. I have studied her, tried to understand why such a feminine card could give me the sense of belonging I had been denying myself for so long. This little account, I hope, will shed some light on this for myself. And, for anyone queer or not, cis or trans, who feels the same fear I did.

A BRIEF NOTE ON DECKS

A more inclusive tarot, one which is not exclusively white, straight or cis, has many champions and practioners. These are people who are enriching the witchcraft space with every reading, interpretation, new deck and conversation.

---

1   It is always preferable to ask politely than to assume
2   This third option is a way to simplify ourselves for a cisgender system. For more information on Nonbinary and Genderqueer identities seek out *They/Them/Their* by Eris Young, Jessica Kingsley Publishers, London, 2020

With so many wonderful decks I feel it is important to mention why I have chosen this High Priestess in this deck. The Waite-Smith[3] tarot is the one you will see most often in the media and it is the most accessible in terms of price and ubiquity. I acknowledge that the Waite-Smith deck is not designed for everyone but it is perhaps the easiest to buy when you first become interested in tarot. As such, we cannot ignore its attitudes and assumptions.

A JOURNEY, AN ARCHETYPE

The Fool's Journey is the story of the twenty-two cards of the major arcana. An innocent begins and is met with trials, tribulations, self-discovery and joy. While the cards are numbered, the Fool is not. The Fool then "belongs anywhere in the deck"[4]. There is no correct start, nor is there a correct end.

This is particularly true for queer people. As Cassandra Snow puts beautifully in *Queering the tarot* (2019), they write in reference to The Magician:

"While The Magician is usually seen as an early-stages life card, for queer people, assuming this would be a mistake. It often takes years to feel comfortable presenting as the gender you weren't assigned at birth. It can take many sexual partners to figure out how you fall in terms of sexual identity ..."[5]

The High Priestess is the second card in the major arcana, sitting in opposition with the Magician. She found me early on my journey of acceptance but relatively late in the common narrative of transness and queerness. Perhaps this is why I have

---

3   This tarot is also known as the Rider-Waite deck but the name Waite-Smith will be used throughout this essay to acknowledge the significant work the artist Pamela Coleman Smith contributed to the creation and artistry of this deck
4   Pollock, Rachel, p28
5   Snow, 2019, p.13

spent so much time considering her. She was my first answer to a question that had grown in me for decades.

THE BODY: TEMPLES, PILLARS, POMEGRANATES AND PALM

As much a card of the mind and the subconscious, the High Priestess is also a card of the body.

Trans people are often reduced to our bodies. Trans women, and particularly trans women of colour, face disproportionate amounts of violence that is still excused in many places as being due to their body[6]. In all public spaces trans women's bodies are demonized. The result of which is often violence.

In common understanding the pillars on this card are Boaz and Jachin, which stand outside the Temple of Solomon. It is key, I feel, to understand that these pillars are not holding the roof of the temple they stand at its entrance. They are as much a piece of symbolism to signal to the outside world a sense of importance and power as they are a symbol of maleness.

Apart from the pillars, the body is represented through the pomegranates, the veil, the mouth of the temple behind our Priestess. The blue colour peeking out is water, often associated with birth and rebirth[7]. These interpretations are aggressively bodied and when I first read them I felt uncomfortable. The phallic pillars and the water and opening as being a symbolic representation of a vagina made me feel hollow. This card which is so much about the mind became yet another reflection of the wrongness of my body. Through time I learned to take this interpretation not as a gendered one, but as a symbolic one. We change who we are often, circumstances change us. Discovering the word nonbinary for me was in a way a rebirth. The pomegranate is the fruit of balance and

6   See the prevalence of the trans panic legal defence, which "legitimizes and excuses violent and lethal behavior against members of the LGBTQ+ community." Holden, Alexandra, "The Gay/Trans Panic Defense: What It is, and How to End It", 2019, www.americanbar.org/groups/crsj/publications/member-features/gay-trans-panic-defense/
7   Pollock, p37–8

contradiction – fertility and death, both used in ritual by eating or by being forbidden[8]. It's seeds are sweet but the skin surrounding them bitter. Seen in myths and legends like the tale of Persephone the fruit is a famous betrayer.

Patterned with the pomegranate on the veil are palm leaves, jagged and well-known as a symbol of victory and strength. Though some interpretations read these as masculine, I instead see them as a symbol of growth through adversity. The palm is a tree of many varieties, the Egyptian palm's dawn pollination is considered to be the birth of the legend of the phoenix, "the mythical bird reborn in a cloud of fire, smoke and ashes in the palm fronds."[9] We know that raising the palm was a symbol of triumph and rebirth in Egyptian art. It is a tree that grows in the warmest and driest climates, it provides fruit and shade. Much like every trans person I know. We are palms. We grow in fire, are reborn in dawn's smoke and shade others from its wrath.

The veil covered in pomegranates and palm leaves is a beautiful representation of the barrier between the conscious and subconscious but also the balance of adversity and strength. The bittersweet of life and death, The High Priestess acknowledges gender but is much more interested in what lies beyond that.

AFTER SEEING, WE LOOK

When reading the tarot for yourself or for others, I urge you to look beyond the title on the card and to examine the images that stand out to you or your subject. Here we can find some of our most important insights.

Everyone has values, cultures, upbringings that place a different lens onto the world. When we read tarot we cannot expect the person we read for to have our same life experiences. In that way, centring the subject and asking for their insights is a wonderful way of being inclusive to trans and cis subjects alike.

---

8 Taschen, p176
9 Wilkinson, p29

WE BORROW, WE MAKE

The religious imagery borrowed from the world is particularly obvious on this card. The High Priestess wears a Christian cross, which draws the eye to the center of the card and her body. She is in a robe that is something between a nun's habit and a Pope's cassock. The cross is dominant to some, while the headdress (similar to that of the ancient Egyptian Goddess of motherhood Hathor) or the Tora will resonate more with others. I see a borrowing from religious institutions; I see her sitting between the pillars; and I see how soft yet strong she looks between them.

Our Priestess can be seen as guarding the subconscious, the spiritual. She sits in contrast to the monoliths of religion, expectation, gender – these societal norms which can dominate and demean us, or give us power and joy. Does she not look so peaceful surrounded by them? She has an insight of what connects them and she promises that you can know too. She invites you to sit with her and think.

In this card, we see the accoutrements of religion represented, the objects are different but the form of religion and of worship is the same. The High Priestess wears the symbols of the powerful and the spiritual yet she is not a court card who collects pentacles or swords. In her role, she has access to the power that connects these spiritual, temporal and bodied images.

THE GREAT BEYOND

My most recent personal discovery in Smith's artwork for this card is, perhaps, the one I value most.

Look to the hem of our Priestess's robes. Is it not reminiscent of sea spray? The crescent moon's reflection is visible over those fabric waves. She may watch over the veil but she also lets part of the great beyond slip through. She does not look uncomfortable; in fact, she is placid. The waves are lapping at the priestesses feet and on the edges of her gown but they are not pulling her in or under. She is steady against the current. The lands and sea beyond the veil are not grasping at her. The High Priestess knows, as many of us do, that they are a part of her.

At twenty seven, and sitting at the kitchen table of a dear friend, I first acknowledged I didn't think I would make it this far. Much like the High Priestess I had spent my life feeling the lapping waves and salt spray of whatever was next. Unlike our Priestess, I felt the water rising with increasing urgency.

For many trans people, the idea of making it to twenty-five, to thirty, to forty or beyond can feel like a fantasy. Each day alive and in ourselves is precious because of the mental health effects of living in a hostile society and the physical violence many face – particularly trans women of colour – as well as being aware of our suicide rates and the prevalence of violence we face[10]. We stand with two feet in death. It is very difficult to participate in divination magic when you cannot see your own future as more than a slither of a possibility.

The High Priestess represents this for me with her feet in the waves, body and mind in the practice of balance, self understanding, a calmness and nonconformity in the face of the pillars of society – religion, establishment and outward strength.

When I asked the cards "What am I fighting?", they did not indicate death as I expected. They said you are in a society in which your being is not acknowledged. Do not turn away from it, you are not fighting the world, you are part of it.

"QUEER NEGOTIATION"

Being nonbinary in witchcraft can be tricky. In his study of queer witchcraft, Martin Lepage proposes "queer negotiations" – these compromises queer people need to make in order to participate in witchcraft[11], particularly in a communal practice.

---

10 In 2020 alone a quarter of trans people had experienced or been threatened with physical assault and more than half felt less able to leave their homes. Dr Cerys Bradley, "Transphobic Hate Crime Report 2020", Galop, 2020
11 Lepage, Martin, "Queerness and Transgender Identity: Negotiations in the Pagan Community of Montreal", *Studies in Religion*, 2017

My negotiation is divine genders. Some of the practices and symbolism of Paganism, Wicca and tarot are heteronormative at best and bioessentialist at worst. This is not always from a place of bigotry, it is a product of the society that many of our traditions were built in. Luckily, many queer people and allies have taken what they need and expanded upon it.

Of course, I do not want to dismiss divine genders – it is a core part of many people's worship and it works for lots of queer people too. They find that representing Pagan (or other) deities as feminine or masculine set in opposition or in harmony with each other to be a key aspect in their rituals or worship. In Wicca, for example, there are roles in ritual for the High Priest and Priestess traditionally portrayed by a man and a woman. But, it can take negotiation. How could I, someone who did not see themselves in the Divine feel comfortable with the worship of such?

> *"The tarot is a question and answer medium, a call and response, a song."*

I do hear a lot about balance, whether from fellow practitioners or card interpretations. And, how balance comes from forces that are at odds: negative and positive, male and female, conscious and subconscious … this world is so often split into twos. To make our practice more open to queer people like me, it takes an openess to a range of experiences, an understanding that the world does not balance with one of each thing – it is not Noah's ark and cannot be divided as such.

WHO ARE YOU FIGHTING FOR?

The tarot is a question and answer medium, a call and response, a song. As you grow as a reader, each strand of interpretation becomes a chord, becomes rhythm, becomes harmony. Becomes story. However, as a medium for justice, inclusion and activism, it can feel small and inadequate.

The High Priestess can seem unrelated to justice movements too, she is so internally focused and lacks the action of the Magician or the demands of Justice. No one card or practice can replace the actions of protest. For trans people in the UK right now we need help accessing very real things such as healthcare, housing, and working rights. Mutual aid groups, protests and petitions are vital to change. This does not mean the tarot and our wider practice has no place in our activism.

Tarot is a strong tool for learning and self-reflection. So often it allows us to acknowledge what we already know in a way that feels safer and more real than simply thinking it. If you feel uncomfortable with queer and/or trans people, ask the cards and yourself why? Examine those thoughts in your own time and use that as a jumping off point to get educated.

If you think you may be queer or trans, speak to the cards about it. They cannot tell you yes or no, but if you are lucky, they may just say exactly what you need to hear.

For those of us who have found who we are right now, the cards can be a space to reaffirm our own intuition. As queer and trans people our internal voice can be so easily drowned out by the world around us.[12] The tarot is a beautiful way to reconnect with that voice.

When reading for others, particularly queer and trans people, you may need to centre an experience vastly different from your own. One which does not conform to traditional interpretations of the cards and may not sit perfectly within the journey of the major arcana. It may seem obvious, but this is what we do for any reading that is not for ourselves.

Trans people so often just want to be seen as they are. In rituals, allow for the trans person to take the position they feel most comfortable in. In readings stress that the gender on the card is not a one-to-one mapping onto the people in their lives. Getting pronouns right and not asking invasive questions

---

12 Snow, p15

is the basic level of respect that we need. We may not correct you, but we do notice.

WHO AM I FIGHTING FOR?

Transition is an act of joy. I am locked in a challenge against those massive dominant structures and so the High Priestess secures me. She holds me in my understanding and encourages me to grow. When I ask if I am trans, she tells me I am worth fighting for. When I feel despair, she lets what is next lap at my feet in waves of ocean. It is okay to acknowledge it is there, she tells me, but it cannot drown you today.

The High Priestess told me what was true inside. I now must embrace the Fool and move forward. My story is early in its telling but I am now so much more open to the world.

And, the future of witchcraft must embrace the unknown too. We need a witchcraft that not only accepts transness as a statement but protects trans people as an action in our everyday practice.

To my trans siblings I say this. The tarot is a symbolic medium and in symbolism, transness can often feel like an

oppositional state, much like witchcraft. This is not the case, being trans and practising magic are not oppositional to the world. Both acknowledge all experiences of living. And both ideas created a space for me to live happily and to bring others in. I hope our craft will do this for you, too.

REFERENCES

Bradley, Cerys, "Dr. Transphobic Hate Crime Report 2020". *Galop*, 2020, https://galop.org.uk/resource/transphobic-hate-crime-report-2020/

Christof, Catherine, *Feminist Action in and through Tarot and Modern Occult Society: The Hermetic Order of the Golden Dawn*, UK and *The Builders of Adytum*, USA. La Rosa di Paracelso, 2017,

Holden, Alexandra, "The Gay/Trans Panic Defense: What It is, and How to End It", www.americanbar.org/groups/crsj/publications/member-features/gay-trans-panic-defense/ 2019.

Lepage, Martin, "Queerness and Transgender Identity: Negotiations in the Pagan Community of Montreal", *Studies in Religion*, vol. 46, 2017

Plymouth College of Art, "Transgender magic and the tarot with pro Rachel Pollack", *YouTube*, 12 May 2021 www.youtube.com/watch?v=FXMGFsg3Rzc&ab_channel=PlymouthCollegeOfArt

Pollock, Rachel, *Seventy Eight Degrees of Wisdom*, Revised edition, Thorstons, London, 1997

Ed. Ronnberg, Ami and Kathleen Martin, "The Archive for Research in Archetypal Symbolism", *The Book of Symbols: Reflections on Archetypal Images*, Taschen, Cologne, 2010

Snow, Cassandra, *Queering the Tarot*, Weiser Books, Newburyport, 2019

Wilkinson, Richard H, *Reading Egyptian Art*, London, 1992

Young, Eris, *They/Them/Their: A Guide to Nonbinary and Genderqueer Identities*, Jessica Kingsley Publishers, London, 2020

"*I was at a spiritual juncture in my life that required me to connect with my higher self.*"

13

YOU CANNOT HEAL OTHERS UNTIL YOU HEAL YOUR OWN "STUFF"
A REFLECTION ON HINDU ARCHETYPES AND SELF-HEALING THROUGH THETAHEALING®

BY BRIANA PEGADO

"*Y*ou cannot heal others until you heal your own stuff" is my ThetaHealing® Master Jennifer Main's[1] mantra and the underlying message of her teachings. It is the underlying message of all ThetaHealing® teaching.

In 2017, I was burned out, exhausted, and had just survived an abusive relationship. I had been living with my partner for almost 18 months up until that point and our break up resulted in a spell of hidden homelessness for months. I was hidden homeless, my visa status was uncertain, and I had just been through an incredibly destabilizing period of my career – finishing up the third year of a festival I set up and ran for three years that had financially impoverished me. Every aspect of my life had been disrupted, upended and undermined in many

---

1   Main, Jennifer. 'Here I am.' www.withjennifer.com/about

ways. I was at a spiritual juncture in my life that required me to connect with my higher self.

A dear friend of mine hosted a work leaving do from an organization I was deeply connected to in the arts in Edinburgh. I dragged myself to the party knowing that seeing some familiar faces would be worthwhile. That night I was introduced to theta healing as an energy healing practice and a shaman I would spend the next four months working with. My friend had been struggling with fertility and had tried everything until she spoke to a fellow artist. This artist and shaman asked her if she had heard of theta energy healing. At this stage my friend had tried everything from meditation to reiki to acupuncture to conceive and she was willing to give anything that might help her on her fertility journey a go. The artist and shaman explained to her that theta healing is a form of energy healing similar to reiki. Theta energy healers channel theta brain waves, rather than alpha brain waves, which reiki healing masters use, or delta brain waves, which we sink into while we are in REM sleep to heal stuck energy and physical ailments. Only reiki healers channel alpha brain wave energies to heal the body, whereas theta healers channel theta brain waves to heal the body. There is also no need to touch or be near the recipient of healing to channel the energy to the body. Reiki healers also perform distance healing with recipients' consent, but often reiki healers will use their palms to scan their clients' bodies to shift energy.

AN INTRODUCTION TO THE THETAHEALING® TECHNIQUE

Theta Healing or The ThetaHealing® Technique was channelled into the world by Vianna Stibal. Stibal describes ThetaHealing® as a spiritual philosophy and meditation technique that she developed after witnessing her own healing over 20 years ago. She describes the energy healing as impacting and healing core DNA patterns. Her discovery that emotions and beliefs affect us on a core, genetic, history and soul level, which is where the

ThetaHealing® technique actively works.[2] It is through healing these core beliefs, which can exist on any or all of these levels of existence that illnesses and ailments can be healed. Theta incorporates talk therapy techniques, guided meditation, past life regression and psychic channelling into its technique to help the healer channel theta energy to the beneficiary of the healing.

The shaman I met that evening shared a reading with me – a message from my guides and ancestors. The message was that I was at a spiritual turning point in my life. She offered her details in case I wanted to work with her at this juncture in my journey with the occult. I emailed her shortly after that and before I knew it, I was in my first session with her. Over four months we worked through medicine wheels, shamanic visualizations, and journeying, my relationship to the Divine, the universe and the occult began to shift. For the first time in my life I was investing the time and energy into my practice with laser focus.

My higher self was waiting for me in my first theta healing session. Her aura was illuminated bright pink. She had long flowing hair and she exuded power, light and energy. She radiated knowledge and wisdom. When the link was activated between me and my higher self, I felt a well of energy unlock. It was like being filled with an overwhelming sense of abundance. I was journeying into a state of euphoria. I remember the feeling of floating into the studio toward my desk at a world-renowned national arts organization I was working for at the time and my boss noticed immediately how different I looked. She told me, I looked calm, serene and whatever I was doing, it suited me. That higher self session was the first of an intensive four-month period of healing sessions, training and shamanic rituals I experienced with the theta healer, shaman and artist I met at the party.

Though I had grown up in love with tarot and astrology, my experiences with the world of the occult were sporadic.

2   Stibal, Vianna, "About Vianna Stibal – Founder of ThetaHealing®", www.thetahealing.com/about-vianna-stibal-founder.html

"We knew we were sitting on the grounds of the most haunted hotel in the city and what we'd seen was not of this world"

I bought my first Thoth tarot deck when I was 12 or 13. My friend Leslie and I would do readings for each other, pull cards and study the deck. One day after school, the two of us were sitting in the grass near the Omni Shoreham Hotel in Washington, DC. The famous mural of Marilyn Monroe painted on the side of a building winked behind us in Woodley Park. While we were lounging in the grass, we both looked up to see a man approaching us in the distance. He was dressed in a simple black suit with a white shirt that had a grandad collar, and he was wearing a black, wide-rimmed hat. He was walking barefoot. We looked away one moment and the next, when we looked back, he was gone. We gave each other a quizzical look and then nodded in response. We had both seen him. We knew we were sitting on the grounds of the most haunted hotel in the city and what we'd seen was not of this world, but a remnant of a spirit from the beyond. Not fully formed in this world, but potentially trapped between the veils.

AN INITIATION

Little did I know in 2017 that my sessions with Eileen would be an initiation of sorts. However, looking back on that year, I realize that the initiation had started a few months before my time with Eileen. It had started in February, with my plea to thegoddess Kali. In school I studied comparative religion, but not the type you might imagine. Though we explored the similarities of the "People of the book" – the teachings of the Abrahamic religions – we also studied the origins of many branches of Hinduism and Buddhism. I became fascinated by Hindu concepts of time and of the Trimurti, which is essentially a trinity of deities that support the existence of the universe: the creator (Brahma), the preserver (Vishnu) and the destroyer (Shiva). The "three forms" work together to sustain the universe or source energy, though the Trimurti is more complex than this, and those who believe in it say it is as diverse as the many branches of Hinduism itself.

This similarity to Christianity – of three forms working together to sustain the source or acting as God like the Holy Trinity – is limited, with Hindu concepts of time and the time cycles (or age) of the universe actually being very different. Whereas in Abrahamic traditions like Christianity, Islam and Judaism, there is no specific measurement of ages nor years that accompany them. Take Hinduism for example, where timelines for the universe and the universal cycles or ages are called Yugas, which are also divine years or years of the universal spirit. The last Yuga or age of time, which is the shortest of a four Yuga cycle, is said to last 432,000 years (1,200 divine years).[3] The precision with which these cycles of time are measured floored and delighted me. These ages can be symbolized by a bull – a sacred animal in Hinduism for many reasons. The bull of dharma (the eternal and inherent nature of reality)[4], has four legs, each representing an age or Yuga. The Yugas are all specific lengths of time with distinct characteristics and varying degrees of peace or discord. The fourth Yuga is the shortest and final age, when the bull of dharma is standing on one foot: this is the age that we are currently in, The Kali Yuga. Named after Goddess Kali or Durga – the bringer of death, destruction, transformation and rebirth – this age is one of discord, destruction and death leading to rebirth into a golden age. The goddess Kali is the goddess of time and part of the chief of the Mahavidyas, ten goddesses who each form different aspects to the mother goddess, Parvati.

---

3   "Kali Yuga", *Wikipedia*, https://en.wikipedia.org/wiki/Kali_Yuga
4   Dharma definition from "Characteristics" of the Yuga Cycle, www.wikipedia.org/wiki/Yuga_Cycle

In early 2017, I read a piece [5] that described an incantation one can say to call in the goddess Kali to destroy and cut the cords of anything not serving you in your life. There were several particular days Kali could be summoned by this incantation. Many of them fell at the beginning of the year in January or February. The day I read the article happened to be one of those particular days. There were a set number of days this chant could be recited, which needed to be on dates significant to the numbers associated with Kali.

I remember lying in bed with my eyes closed, reciting the words. Nothing happened at first, but the week that followed spelled absolute disaster.

Once summoned, Kali was exacting, ruthless and thorough. She left nothing untouched or behind from her purging. She was the demon slayer. A few weeks after summoning the Goddess, my life had transformed. I was free from my ex, my things were in storage, I had taken a month off on holiday and though I had no idea where I was going next, toxic relationships had evaporated from my life. It all happened quite suddenly, but it felt like exactly how Kali's influence had been described. The cords were cut and it had not been easy. Though I was facing a future of uncertainty, I had the power to choose my own destiny.

> "A few weeks after summoning the Goddess, my life had transformed."

It is a funny thing having the courage to change your circumstances when you know you are not living in alignment with your values – when you know you are not living with integrity. I knew deep down that the life I had built for

5   Myles, Alex. "2017 is The Year of Kali, Goddess of Endings & Beginning", *Elephant Journal*, www.elephantjournal.com/2017/01/2017-is-the-year-of-kali-goddess-of-endings-beginnings/

myself up until that point was a life I was living out of my own power not grounded deeply in it. It had the veneer of the life I desired. I was doing creative work while I would spend my evenings in the shower hearing a voice in my head anxiously questioning whether I was in the right relationship. I was making my own way in the world in a city I loved and I was being recognized for my accomplishments, but I was overworked and tired. Everything felt like a performance and I was not happy, not truly happy.

Since my first experience of working with her, it feels like whenever I am act out of alignment with myself Durga (Goddess Kali) comes right back in to wreak havoc and destruction. It can feel quite explosive at times, but she simply does not waste any time. She takes no prisoners. As time has passed and I have learned to understand when things are out of alignment, I am able to steer myself back on course gently and Kali has less reason to appear with her exacting fury. I also made sure to thank Kali for her work and stop the invocation, so that any new shifts are a result of my own actions.

HEAL YOUR OWN "STUFF"

I completed my ThetaHealing® Basic Training in 2018 and it through this work that I have started to see my past experiences from a different perspective. I find that I have an uncanny ability to see dysfunction in most situations. In work environments this might be dysfunction in team structures, professional relationships, management or the mission of an organisation. I see organizations, companies and projects as living, breathing organisms with their own auras. In some ways my uncanny ability and gift to see dysfunction is really my way of performing an energy reading or aura scan on these organisms. It is only recently I have understood what was happening. Think of these scans as an automatic reading that calibrates with my body and sends out a signal. This would happen in real time without any effort and often would result in conflict, clashes or big drama in workplaces. It was as if my energy fundamentally clashed with the energy of those around me or the company itself.

These clashes often emerged as problems or conflicts within the organization, which I would share with management. When I have shared what I've learned through these "energy readings," it often unearths deep-held truths about a situation that seemed obvious to me but were fundamentally disruptive to the listener. To speak truth to power to the individuals creating the dysfunction in these organizations is challenging. It was even more challenging when I did not realize it would not be well-received. Those truths would often confront people about their actions, complicity and behaviour to maintain their positions. It was often an abuse of power they did not recognize or acknowledge. Often, I am a disrupting presence in these settings and over the years it has become part of my modus operandi – unearthing and healing toxic dynamics in the world of work. No longer do I see these situations as dynamics that find me, any more than energy imbalances I have been put on this earth to help rebalance – to help root out toxicity.

WHY IT IS IMPORTANT TO "HEAL OUR OWN STUFF"

Often what we see out in the world is a reflection of our own "baggage", "trauma", "deep-held beliefs", "limiting beliefs", and "dysfunctions". In psychology, we often refer to this phenomenon as our "projections".[6] What I pick up in work settings and partnerships is no different. It is a reflection of what is dysfunctional within me. This is why healing our "own stuff", as Jennifer puts it, is so important. Through shifting stuck energy, clearing chakras, resolving trauma through limiting beliefs held by ancestors, theta energy healing allows us to do the deep work to release trauma. We are often speaking to others with and being led by our trauma/hurt rather than being guided by our healthy experiences. If we do not address our own beliefs shaped by

6   "It's Not Me, It's You: Projection Explained in Human Terms", Projection Psychology, *Healthline*, https://www.healthline.com/health/projection-psychology

past trauma, we continue to impose harm on others. That is why it is so important for us to heal ourselves in order to prevent ourselves from projecting our traumas onto others. Otherwise, we live in a space of continuous energetic word vomit that we just spew onto others unconsciously. It is not like this work will be finished in our lifetime because healing is not linear nor does it reach an endpoint. Vianna believes, like many other healers, that if we have the courage to heal as aspect of ourselves in this lifetime, the healing travels back down our ancestral line and heals all of our ancestors.

"Healing Your Own Stuff" in a modern world of inter-connectedness and hyper-globalization is now a more accessible process than ever. With the rise of modern astrology, a multi-billion pound wellness industry, internet activism, an acknowledgement of the importance of intersectionality when addressing global oppression, and trauma-informed work, there are a plethora of ways to address unresolved trauma. I always look at the modernization of healing from a sustainable development and design-thinking perspective. Now, what do I mean? Sustainable development is a discipline of looking at environmental degradation – including, but not limited to, the climate crisis – from an economic, social and political standpoint. It draws on wisdom across disciplines, philosophies and wisdom traditions, centring deeply ecological earth knowledge as a means of saving us from the impending climate crisis in ways that are post-capitalist.

> *"The occult and our relationship to it is changing ..."*

Now we're living through late-stage capitalism. Mass burnout, mental ill-health, and climate crisis have led to an increased interest in wellness, which has fuelled the growth of the wellness industry. More nuanced conversations around what we require as a species for survival are emerging. The occult and our relationship to it is changing: in some ways one could argue it is re-emerging. In the field of spiritual ecology, this shift in perspective and re-emergence of our relationship to the Divine is also known as The Great or Third Turning, a phrase coined by Joanna Macy [7]. Spiritual ecologists believe this is a turning point and a paradigm shift that will allow humans to restore our relationship to nature. I see this turning taking place in the rise in popularity and return to witchcraft, people honouring the wheels of the year, crystal work, candle magic, ritual work, altar setting, modern astrology and the use of tarot.

Tony Fry, an Australian design and systems thinker and environmentalist, purports that we are moving from the "Age of Enlightenment" to the "Age of Sustainment". [8] An age that will require us to look our problems in the eye and tackle them head on to guarantee our future; an age where we will design a future in harmony with the earth that is sustainable for all species on it. I believe that looking at our problems directly requires us to heal ourselves by staring our trauma in the face. So much of what I see emerging in this time of transition, during this Kali Yuga, is a result of unresolved trauma. Whether generational, intergenerational, familial or social, our inability to have collective conversations about healing trauma as a society is what is causing a lot of our suffering. The good news is that there is an incredibly large number of people doing this healing work to heal themselves and others, and therefore heal our relationship to one another – and to the planet.

HEALING IN THE MODERN WORLD

In their community, for communities, in secret or out in the open, healers are stepping forward. Healers have always been a huge part of our society: protecting us, guiding us and helping us move forward through great uncertainty since the beginning

7   Macy, Joanna, "Joanna Macy: The Great Turning is a shift from the Industrial Growth Society to a life-sustaining civilization", www.ecoliteracy.org/article/great-turning
8   Fry, Tony, "Design As Politics, Foreward", 1 November 2010

of time, or at least since we became sentient beings. There is no greater example of where healers have found community than the healing community formed online through social media.

Not only has social media unlocked knowledge, concepts, discussions, self-care methods, soothing practices, critical discourse and deeply sacred ritual for the masses, it has helped create a greater community around care. We must remember, however, that social media is a tool that is neither inherently good nor bad, but it can be used for good or for bad depending on whoever wields it. While the multi-billion-pound wellness industry has been growing, so has our need to be even more discerning.

People who bring their politics into their wellness and healing spaces can carry incredible biases. The fine line between someone running their own healing practice in the best way they know how and running it while being open to critical reflection can be blurry. There are so many well-meaning practitioners out there who have not done the inner work on themselves before they start helping others. They haven't healed their own "stuff" and they are working outside of integrity because of it. We know healing is a journey and "progress is not linear", as Maria Montessori once said.[9] No one in this life will ever be fully healed. Healing is not about perfection, but awareness, in order to prevent causing unnecessary harm to others.

I have been in spaces I thought were safe and healing until a healing practitioner made a comment that lifted the veil on their views, along with my safety in proximity to them. A healer I worked with for years made a comment about all of us needing to transcend race and let go of how it divides us. That comment may have been seen as harmless by the group, but as the only black woman in the healing space, I felt my very real experience of racism was being trivialized. That lack of acknowledgement may seem small, but it is deeply violent. It is a form of privilege that reinforces the erasure of all of the other black women in that space.

---

9   Montessori, Maria, 1946 Lecture in London, "Progress is not linear", www.montessorieducation.com/blog/progress-is-not-linear

I sat with this revelation for months because I had to think about whether or not I would confront this healer. I did raiseit, though I knew this was learning and work this healer needed to do on their own, in their own time and with professionals. It was not my job to teach this healer how harmful their beliefs were – especially in a space as sacred as a healing space – when going through that process with them would put me at risk for more intentional or unintentional gaslighting and abuse. The intention of the behaviour does not change its ability to harm.

When someone is confronted with the ways in which they have caused harm I find it often goes one of two ways. They feel shame and get defensive, all the while finding places to shift blame to make themselves feel better. Or they take on the feedback as learning and transmute their discomfort in understanding they have caused harm into a learning they take with them into the future. The latter requires the strength and courage of the Goddess Kali. It requires the integrity of looking a problem in the eye – a thing that Tony Fry recommends if we are to transition into an Age of Sustainment. Both of these actions are fundamental for our collective healing, but require personal discomfort and sacrifice.

Spiritual bypassing is a fascinating thing. The denial of harm at the expense of marginalized groups, from which – in the case of the healing community – many healing teachings originate feels particularly ironic and harmful. Pointing out this type of spiritual harm often occurs through the emotional labour of minority groups that have experienced the harm of the bypassing in the first place, like in my earlier example. If someone's healing practice is not inclusive and perpetuates harm through dismissing lived experiences of others – or if it appropriates cultures not only not the healer's own, but if credit is taken for it being their own – not honouring the source of these teachings as wisdom from indigenous communities and communities of colour, then the harm, erasure, and colonialism in these spaces continues.

TAKING RESPONSIBILITY FOR OUR OWN CORNER OF THE WORLD

I write this piece from a land that is not my own, by nature of it not being my place of birth. It is my chosen home – for now. I've understood my responsibility to make a contribution to this place I call home, to this society. I think back to a visit to Sedona, Arizona when I was 20 years old. I came into contact with a spiritual guide and healer who was our tour guide in the desert. We had a long conversation about synchronicities, spiritual encounters, belief systems and things I remembered from past lives. We visited the town of Jerome, which hosted the most haunted hotel in the United States. I walked in, took one whiff and could smell the remnants of an old folks' home. The stench was overwhelming – so overwhelming I had to leave the building. I waited outside and the guide came back out with my mother. "What happened?" He asked. I explained. He then said, "You know this was an old persons' home before it became a hotel. You smelled its previous existence. Has anyone ever told you that you are clairalient[10]? You have the psychic smell or in other words 'clear smelling'?" I thought back on many experiences I'd had as a child and I was not surprised. It took one stranger who could recognize my skills for what they were to put me on a path to having a better knowledge of myself.

If the places we live and people we live among act as a mirror for us to better ourselves, to better know ourselves, to heal our stuff, the question is what role will you play? How will you honour the place you live? If it is a giant mirror, do you dare look at your own reflection?

---

10 "Clairealience", *Wiktionary*, https://en.wiktionary.org/wiki/clairalience

GIANTS, WEAVERS AND OTHER BODIES

"The witch-hunts that took place in early modern Europe could be considered one of the only mass genocides in history to be widely reduced to an aesthetic."

14

GIANTS, WEAVERS AND OTHER BODIES

BY MEGAN RUDDEN

*T*he witch-hunts that took place in early modern Europe could be considered one of the only mass genocides in history to be widely reduced to an aesthetic. While written records concerning the victims of the witch-hunts may be hard to come by, visual depictions of these women are cemented so deeply in our collective imagination, that most people can easily recall the image of a witch. While the artists who first conjured these fantastical images have performed a vital role in the creation of the witch as a malevolent character, in reducing her to the binary of old hag/young temptress, the contemporary artists I will consider in this essay have offered a feminist reimagining of the multiplicity of images possible under the title of "witch". Central to this discussion will be the work of Georgia Horgan, Jesse Jones and Linda Stupart, as examples of contemporary artists working with depictions of the witch who have attempted to reconcile not only her image, but the resistance possible in her existence. I will consider the text *Caliban and the Witch: Women, the Body and Primitive Accumulation*, by radical autonomist Marxist feminist Silvia Federici, which traces the history of the body within the "transition" from feudalism to capitalism, considering how the witch-hunts that took place in early modern Europe were a fundamental component to early capitalist development.[1]

---

1   Federici, Silvia, 2004

The arrival of second-wave feminism sparked the critical re-emergence of the witch, in relation to issues of class, gender and the treatment of the labouring body under patriarchal capitalism. The witch-hunt remains one of the most understudied events in European history,[2] and the necessity for further evaluation of this time period may account for a resurgence in contemporary art practices considering the oppression of the witch. As Anne Barstow notes in *Witchcraze: A New History of the European Witch Hunts*, many historians studying this period have neglected to fully examine the gendered power relations that instigated this genocide, failing to recognize misogyny and patriarchy as valid historical categories.[3] Barstow concludes that in refusing to treat "women" as a term to define a particularly oppressed group or class within capitalism at this time, historians have avoided a sufficiently critical gender analysis of the witch-hunts. Because of this historical invisibility, it is useful to consider "women", in relation to other marginalized genders and oppressed groups, to fully understand the political effects of the witch-hunts, and their lasting impact in the creation of gender ideology. Barstow suggests that 85 per cent of those killed for the crime of "witchcraft" were women[4] and Federici concurs that the witch-hunts were "a war against women" created to "degrade them, demonize them, and destroy their social power."[5]

The definition of women as demonic beings, and the atrocious and humiliating practices to which so many on them were subjected left indelible marks on the collective female psyche … From every viewpoint – socially, economically, culturally, politically, – the witch-hunt was a turning point in women's lives … [it] destroyed a whole world of female practices, collective relations and systems of knowledge.[6]

---

2   Federici, Silvia, p163
3   Barstow, Anne Llewellyn, p4
4   Barstow, Anne Llewellyn
5   Federici, Silvia, p186
6   Federici, Silvia, p103

Accounts of the sadistic forms of torture, and the sexual nature of these, used against women accused of witchcraft exposes a period of misogyny unparalleled by any other event in history. A great aid in the dissemination of these tactics was the *Malleus Maleficarum* (*The Hammer of Witches*) written by a Catholic clergyman.[7] It was one of the most widely read books at the time, second only to the Bible in terms of sales for almost two hundred years. The *Malleus* was a mass-distributed instruction manual,[8] which depicts in horrific, torturous and deeply pornographic detail the correct procedure to follow on discovery of a "witch". The text is littered with fantastical castration-anxiety fuelled stories, such as witches who stole a collection of penises to hang in a tree like phallic fruit. It was not long before these well-circulated, highly visual descriptions of witch practices entered the imagination of an art world dominated by men depicting women.[9]

While some of the earliest sixteenth century imagery of the witch can be attributed to Albrecht Dürer, it was not a theme that entirely dominated his work. One of his students, on the other hand, zealously took up the task of imagining the witch in the most appalling of scenes. The woodcuts created by Hans Baldung Grien were abundant in devil copulation, erotic rituals and bulging bodies that rode broomsticks through the night. Baldung's rich iconography and compositional finesse gave this world credibility, yet made clear its underlying principles of irrationality, gullibility, bestial sexuality,

---

7   Although later banned by the Catholic Church in 1490

8   The *Malleus* was printed in a particularly small size for that time, convenient for carrying in a pocket

9   Another early text on witchcraft was Ulrich Molitor's *De lamiis et pythonicis mulieribus*, arriving soon after the *Malleus Maleficarum*. Although Molitor's treatise expressed more moderate views than the *Malleus*, its imagery offered less scepticism than the text, with one woodcut depicting a witch embracing an Incubus demon. From 1489 to 1669, more copies of Molitor's text were printed than the *Malleus* itself. As Federici notes, "Alerting the public to the dangers posed by the witches was one of the first tasks of the printing press", – Federici, Silvia, p168

> "The woodcuts created by Hans Baldung Grien were abundant in devil copulation, erotic rituals and bulging bodies"

malevolence and apostasy. The confrontation staged by these drawings would be echoed in the witch-hunts.[10]

That these images were among the first visual representations of the witch to be seen, not only by the general public, but also the jurors and early Reformers, would have been extremely powerful in shaping initial attitudes toward her. As Federici states, the witch-hunt was the first persecution in Europe to make use of "multi-media propaganda" to cause large-scale "psychosis among the population".[11] Therefore, alongside the jurors who condemned, the church that cried devil worship, the state that orchestrated mass murder and the executioner who lit the fires, must sit the artists who first visually imagined her image.

One artist attempting to counter this oppressive history through critical re-evaluation of the witch-hunts is Glasgow-based artist Georgia Horgan, who has taken explicit influence from the work of Silvia Federici. Through *Machine Room*, an exhibition that took place in 2015 at Collective gallery, Edinburgh, Horgan applied a research model initiated by Federici to examine acute periods of witch-hunting in Scotland and their relationship to the development of industry.[12] Horgan found that there was a direct correlation between areas of intense industrialization and high rates of witch burnings, stating that East Lothian "was the most dangerous place to be a woman in this era, after Essex" due to its connection to the

10 Hults, Linda C, p91
11 Federici, Silvia, p168
12 Collective, Edinburgh, Georgia Horgan: *Machine Room*, 14 February–19 April 2015

expansive weaving industry throughout the Scottish borders.[13] As Federici noted, it was significant that the majority of the witch trials in England took place in Essex, as by the sixteenth century most of the land in that area had been enclosed, connecting the effects of land privatization and loss of the commons to increased levels of witch-hunting.[14] Horgan re-contextualizes this information by presenting it in the gallery space, questioning the way history is represented.[15] Digitally knitted tapestries depict graphs of witch-hunting accusations in rural areas against accusations in industrialized areas, making visual the stark correlation between witch-hunting and industrialization while eluding to the history of the textile industry and the implications of new technologies. An array of research material is laid out on a table, and gaps cut into the surface of the wood suggest the possibility of accommodating a sewing machine.

As both Horgan and Federici demonstrate, it is necessary to consider the wider socio-economic conditions of the time as major instigating factors of the witch-hunt. Persecution of witches peaked during the "transition" period from feudalism to capitalism, yet as Federici argues, this was not a natural progression but a newly enforced order created through violence, subjugation and enslavement, a counter reaction to the building power of proletarian revolts. During the witch-hunting era, living conditions were dire; many endured extreme poverty, and plague and illness were rife. The expropriation of the peasantry created a shortage of land and food production, which resulted in mass hunger and the appearance of a new vagrant "underclass", amplified by the ever-growing population. At the same time, rapid colonial

13 Georgia Horgan interviewed by Izabella Scott, "Georgia Horgan: Confident, working women were a threat to the social order," *Studio International*, 24 May 2017, www.studiointernational.com/index.php/georgia-horgan-interview-all-whores-are-jacobites

14 Federici, Silvia, p171

15 Centre for Contemporary Arts Glasgow, Georgia Horgan in conversation with Ainslie Roddick, *Vimeo*, August 2016, https://vimeo.com/170498977

expansion into the Americas was creating a surplus of cheap labour through the exploitation of enslaved people, while the merchant class enjoyed the prosperity of imported gold and silver, leading to rising rates of inflation. This growing disparity of wealth between the rich and the poor fuelled accusations of witchcraft within the lower classes, as charges included begging, stealing and "cursing" ones neighbour for not sharing food supplies. As Federici notes, these "diabolical crimes" were nothing more than "the class struggle played out at the village level".[16]

Jesse Jones examines the ways in which the law transmits memory between generations, with particular interest in how constitutions have affected the treatment of women's bodies. Her work moves across vast time periods, from considering the anthropological discovery of a 3.5-million-year-old female body, to the voices silenced by the witch trials, to present day Ireland and the recent movement to repeal the 8th amendment, giving women the right to a safe abortion.[17] Initially created for the Irish Pavillion at Venice Biennale in 2017, and taking *Caliban and the Witch* as a starting point, Jones' multimedia installation *Tremble Tremble* reimagines the historical implications of the law by proposing the witch as an archetypal figure capable of disrupting histories and transforming reality.

Another influence from Federici can be found in the title of the work, taken from the 1970s "Wages Against Housework" campaign,[18] as the protestors would chant "Tremate tremate, le streghe sono tornate!" (Tremble, tremble, the witches have

---

16 Federici, Silvia, p171

17 It is interesting to note that despite the historical influence of the Church in Irish lawmaking, only four executions of witches took place in Ireland. Federici claims this is due to the "collective land-tenure system and kinship ties" still present there, showing that although Church dogma played a huge role in the creation of the witch as a malevolent character, the with-hunts were essentially political, and directly related to the new capitalist model. – Federici, Silvia, p171

18 Led by Silvia Federici and other feminist activists, including Mariarosa Dalla Costa and Selma James.

returned!). The work proposes a magical, feminist, new world order, in which the only site of true law is the womb of *In Utera Gigantae*, the most giant of witches. Jones creates a mythology that not only draws from her extensive research, but suggests an alternative origin story:

> I was thinking a lot about how you could tell a mythic story that would create a counter to what was happening in and around the law and the female body ... The other thing that was really important to me was to try and think back ... [to] imagine that feminism was two million years old and how could you create a structure of memory through an aesthetic experience that might conjure a collective idea about how we can have agency.[19]

Jones reminds us of the vital fact that feminist politics extend far beyond the beginning of first wave feminism, connecting us through deep time to the histories and struggles of our ancestors. We are reminded of the limitations of thinking of feminism within a linear timeline, or a series of "waves" that implies another limiting temporality, and to consider a feminist politics that stretches beyond in both time and space. *In Utera Gigantae* exists simultaneously before and after the law, yet the viewer encounters her myth in the present, transforming the time-space of the womb – a site of exploitation and control under patriarchal capitalism – into a site of possibility.

During the sixteenth and seventeenth centuries, drastic changes in the law were eroding women's rights, one of the main affects of this being that they lost the right to take part in economic exchanges alone, contributing to their domestication. The charge upon which women were held during the witch-hunts, was incredibly vague, more concerned with the act of witchcraft itself than the supposed consequence

---

19 Talbot Rice Gallery, Jesse Jones: *Tremble Tremble / At The Gates at Talbot Rice Gallery, YouTube,* 27 April 2020, www.youtube.com/watch?v=AaDZOxYcPEw

of its practice, which ultimately was impossible to prove. Witch accusations gave those in power control over even the most ordinary aspects of every day life, and were ultimately used to eliminate a certain type of personality that did not conform to the newly enforced social position for women: unmarried or widowed women who lived alone; poor women who begged for food; and older women who could no longer contribute to the reproduction of the workforce.[20] At the same time, all forms of non-procreative sexuality were demonized. Significantly, during this period, the only charge against women more common than accusations of witchcraft, was infanticide.[21] Federici connects this to a growing concern over the size of the exploitable workforce, further indicated by the introduction of census-taking and severe punishment for "reproductive crimes", such as the death penalty for mothers who aborted their children.

This was echoed in *The Malleus*, which declared the midwife as the single biggest threat among women, as they helped the mother "destroy the fruit of her womb."[22] Through torture, fear and murder, the witch-hunts removed all reproductive control from women, placing it in the hands of the state, a fact that we are yet to recover from. The significance of this event in alienating women from their own bodies in order to exploit them for capitalist gain cannot be underestimated.

The mythology materialized as *In Utera Gigantae* towers over the viewer on huge screens that dominate the gallery space from floor to ceiling. In creating an "aesthetic experience" to enter, Jones offers the possibility of being immersed in an alternative collective memory. Other performative movements and speculative objects also appear in the space; a gigantic bone illuminated momentarily with a spotlight, a circle drawn repeatedly on the wall. As the exhibition moves from pavilion to gallery, the objects are altered and replaced. There is a sense

20 Federici, Silvia, p170
21 Federici, Silvia, p179
22 Federici, Silvia, p183

that this story is not fixed, but in constant motion, reshaped and retold by the people and places that it encounters. In this context, the witch symbolizes the possibility of transformation, of retelling and even reshaping history, a giantess capable of transcending the boundaries of the state and the law, her corporeal being existing long before either.

The giant witch ridicules the courts, and it is clear that Jones too may be distrustful of historical "evidence", perhaps another reason for offering an alternative myth. *In Utera Gigantae* spits the words of *The Malleus Maleficarum* backward, inverting and reclaiming the power of the language once used to incite violence and hatred toward women.

"Through torture, fear and murder, the witch-hunts removed all reproductive control from women"

Similarly, during a performance that took place in 2016 at Tranmission gallery, Glasgow, Linda Stupart and Travis Alabanza amplified their own oppressed voices through the language of witchcraft, to expel from their space words that have been used so violently against them.[23] Together they created a protection spell and, like the witches of the past, made a pact to protect each other from external forces that wish to do them harm.

Although they have both encountered oppression in different forms, they share the experience of existing in bodies that have been othered by the system of white, heteronormative, patriarchal capitalism. They make a salt circle on the floor to create a place where they can exist in safety together, while a sound piece in the background recounts a conversation between the two discussing the

---

23 Stupart, Linda and Travis Alabanza, "A Spell To Protect Each Other", 16 April 2016, performance as part of *Coven* residency, Transmission Gallery, Glasgow

oscillation between invisibility and hyper-visibility through everyday experience. Like Jones, Stupart draws from histories of witchcraft and magic to create narrative structures that allow us to imagine an alternative present, while also considering the possibility of a queer future.

The story of the witch is the history of everybody who has become other, of those who have dared to exist outside the model of capitalist relations as controlled by white, male authority, becoming the ultimate threat of resistance to patriarchal hierarchy. As Federici notes, the systematic torture and massacre of thousands of "witches" would not have taken place on such a widespread scale unless they posed a significant threat to the power structure.[24] The effects of the witch-hunts can still be felt palpably in our daily lives, in the limitations of the gender binary and the current oppressive conditions of late-stage capitalism, as the sexual devision of labour lingers on through wage gaps and precarious working conditions. In realizing the very complex and multifaceted history within which the witch figure is situated, we can better understand the implications of artists working with her image today. These artists have attempted to instigate an alternative narrative through the critical reconsideration of the witch, drawing from her power as a figure of resistance in an attempt to counter a torturous history of misogyny.

---

24 As Barstow confirms, "certain women were suspected of witchcraft, not because they were powerless, but precisely because they were seen to have a great deal of power" – Barstow, Anne Llewellyn, p110

BIBLIOGRAPHY

Barstow, Anne Llewellyn, Witchcraze: A New History of the European Witch Hunts, HarperOne, 1994

Centre for Contemporary Arts Glasgow, Georgia Horgan in conversation with Ainslie Roddick, *Vimeo*, August 2016 https://vimeo.com/170498977

Collective, Edinburgh, Georgia Horgan: *Machine Room*, 14 February–19 April 2015

Federici, Silvia, *Caliban and the Witch: Women, the Body and Primitive Accumulation*, Autonomedia, 2004

Federici, Silvia, *Witches, Witch-hunting and Women*, PM Press, 2018

Gage, Matilda Joslyn, *Women, Church and State*, Arno Press 1973, original 1893

Hults, Linda C. *The Witch as Muse: Art, Gender, Power in Early Modern Europe*, University of Pennsylvania Press, 2005

Horgan, Georgia interviewed by Izabella Scott, "Georgia Horgan: Confident, working women were a threat to the social order," Studio International, 24 May 2017 https:// www.studiointernational.com/index.php/georgia-horgan-interview-all-whores-are-jacobites

Jones, Jesse, *Tremble Tremble* ed. Tessa Giblin, published on the occasion of Ireland at Venice: the Pavilion of Ireland at the 57th Venice Biennale, Dublin: Project Press and Milan: Mousse, 2017

Kramer, Heinrich and Sprenger, Jacob, *Malleus Maleficarum* Translated by Rev. Montague Summers, The Pushkin Press, 1971, original Germany, 1487

Stupart, Linda and Travis Alabanza, "A Spell to Protect Each Other", 16 April 2016, performance as part of *Coven* residency, Transmission Gallery, Glasgow

Monter, E. William, *Courtly Love and Witchcraft published in Becoming Visible: Women in European History*, p.119–136 ed. Renate Bridenthal and Claudia Koonz, Houghton Mifflin, 1977

Talbot Rice Gallery, Edinburgh, Jesse Jones / *Tremble Tremble*, 27 October 2018–26 January 2019

Talbot Rice Gallery, Jesse Jones: *Tremble Tremble / At The Gates* at Talbot Rice Gallery, *YouTube*, 27 April, 2020 www.youtube.com/watch? v=AaDZOxYcPEw

"The story of the witch is the history of everybody who has become other ..."

BUILDING A COSMOLOGY OF ACCESS

"I am an English witch wheeling an Irish pagan path."

15

BUILDING A COSMOLOGY OF ACCESS:
A DAY IN THE LIFE OF A DISABLED LAND-BASED PRACTICE

BY MADELYN BURNHOPE

a: a branch of metaphysics that deals with the nature
of the universe
b: a theory or doctrine describing the natural order of
the universe

from Mirriam-Webster's definition of "Cosmology"

I am an English witch wheeling an Irish pagan path. I am also disabled: born with Spina bifida and Hydrocephalus, later diagnosed with EUPD (Emotionally Unstable Personality Disorder) and depression, and I am a full-time wheelchair user. At a time when Neopagan and Wiccan concepts like "hedge witch" are booming – with their implied pressure to flee the 'trappings' of the very technology that enables our participation in society, and "all mod cons" like disabled toilets, then ramble for miles, foraging along cliffsides, over steep hills, and in ocean rockpools – what happens if we are relegated to the "beaten path", the middle of the road?

What does it mean to have a land-based practice when we can't access the land?

Instead of writing you a "How to Be a Disabled Witch" checklist, or a "Where to Visit if You're in a Wheelchair" cosmic travel article, I want to take you on a journey through a day in the life of my practice, alongside which I've built a "cosmology of access" less concerned with meeting unrealistic abled-centric standards in its details than with forging connections to the land wherever possible, in the knowledge that wherever we sit, we are attached to the land, and conductors of its energy. As we fight for concrete accessible infrastructure and accommodations, magical paths of access to the lands we inhabit and work with are already opening to us.

Disability will be my main focus, but I also write as a white, British-English trans woman, with both a history of Roman colonization, and a heritage as a colonizer of Ireland and the world. So, the right relationship with cultural tradition is the second boot we'll put on before we set off on our journey.

Ready? Let's begin.

HOME AND HEARTH

Since living in my one-bedroom flat, I've filled it with symbols of Irish paganism and witchcraft (two interconnected, though different things; paganism, a belief system, needn't involve witchcraft, and witchcraft is not itself religious). Brick-a-brack to the untrained eye, they are also tools of my connection: if disability prevents me from retrieving the "right" ingredient from nature (a specific flower, say), I find or buy an object that, for me, carries its meaning (such as a bowl painted with that flower). I've come to work with symbolism perhaps more than energy, small gestures rather than elaborate ritual.

Research is my foraging and my first place of connection to the land is in learning: the more I learn, the more precise my visualization, the more discerning my choice of object, the more targeted my magic. So the bookcase in my lounge, small and low enough for me to access from my wheelchair, contains enough books and materials to keep what I'm doing – including this essay – accountable to Irish tradition, along with Kindle books, websites, PDF essays and social media communities.

Next to my bookcase, three small, low tables are altars to my Irish gods: the Morrigan on the left (my largest and most complex altar, as She would have it!); Brigid on the right; the Dagda and the Cailleach in the middle. "The Tuatha De Danann are mainly considered to be the Gods of Ireland",[1] and only one of mine – the Cailleach – is generally outside it. Each altar displays a few objects – mainly bought at charity shops or over the internet – busy doing the magic of symbolic meaning-making. I don't physically interact with these much, due to my fear of falling and knocking things over, but each has a single bowl for offerings. This morning, I sit at my altars giving my Gods praise and thanks, asking them for help with issues involving me, my friends and communities, then drop them an offering in gratitude for hearing me. Tomorrow, I'll either pour them in the bushes outside or discard them in my kitchen bin, with thanks to the gods for receiving them. If they're likely to spill, I'll bring a bin bag to the altar and pour away in situ.

"Fire and water are ubiquitous in Irish culture and tradition."

My lounge has an electric heater with an artificial "bonfire" display. I used it as a focal point for Bealtaine, through to the Summer Solstice. "Bealtaine (pron. Bee-Yowl-tinneh in my standardized Irish, and Bal-tin-eh in some other dialect voices) is still the name in modern Irish for the month of May … the only proper name for the festival in this country, where we have a living linguistic term for it".[2]

---

1 Daimler, 2015
2 O'Brien, 2020

Fire and water are ubiquitous in Irish culture and tradition. I light a candle around the house for all sorts of reasons, but, due to slightly shaky fine motor skills, I use LED candles instead of real ones. And at my kitchen sink, I pour water three times over each of my hands with a miniature jug I've dedicated to Brigid, a small act of devotion and dedication I try to do daily. "She is associated with both fire and water, as her modern Christian equivalent, Saint Brigid, has a perpetual flame and holy well in Kildare".[3] The inner certainty that non-traditional rituals like these "feel right" to me is "UPG" (Unverified Personal Gnosis) but I've built them from what I've learned of the tradition.

Outside my front door is a concrete car park, but before it is a large bed of bushes and shrubs, my own patch of greenery in a town with little except the local park – near to me but up a steep hill – woodland on the outskirts, a couple of lakes and the River Anker, all too far to reach without public transport. Coventry Canal goes through town though, and I spend time there when I can in lieu of any Irish holy wells, soaking in its energy, aware that eventually its water meets and mingles with the Irish sea, and beyond. "It can generally be said that rivers were seen as channels of energy from the Otherworld and associated with specific Goddesses[4]".[5]

> "It can generally be said that rivers were seen as channels of energy from the Otherworld ..."

One bush is growing so hard against my bathroom window that I can't open it without the leafy arms reaching inside. It needs cutting back, but first, what is it? After a quick internet search, I'm almost certain: Rockspray cotoneaster. Native to

3   Daimler, 2015
4   O hOgan, 2006
5   Daimler, 2015

China, it has done well in Britain, as well as Counties Down and Antrim, and the city of Dublin, Ireland. And it's related to the hawthorn and the rowan, both important in Irish tradition. A hawthorn grows alone at the mouth of Uaimh na gCat ("Cave of the Cats"), the "fit abode" of The Morrigan, telling those who enter (on foot, it's far too cramped for wheelchairs) they are about to inhabit an Otherworldly space. Is it possible to have some kind of portal to the Irish Otherworld on English soil? Will I anger any fairies by getting rid of it?[6] Lora O'Brien warns against treating the Aos Sídhe or "Good Neighbours" (two euphemisms among many to avoid speaking the "f"-word) as the twee, sanitized, winged sprites of Victorian art or Disney movies. Morgan Daimler urges caution and balance in dealing with the fairies of Ireland or Britain.

All interesting questions, but I don't yet have enough answers to confidently base UPG on them. For now, it's enough that in minutes, the greenery outside my flat has become a sacred space; a microcosm of all the land around me, near and far, and its energy. I can draw it all in just as a Wiccan might draw down the moon (UPG). As disabled people, we can look for those tiny turning-circles of dirt and leaves, and harness their magic. So, it was on that Rockspray cotoneaster that I hung my Brat Bríd on Imbolg, the time when Brigid is celebrated; and from another bush that I picked yellow flowers to scatter over my threshold for protection from fairies on the Summer Solstice. Today, I simply sit and meditate on all my greenery for a while, before wheeling down my ramp for a quick visit to town. I have a plan.

TOWN AND COUNTY

I know no spells or rituals to make high hills flat, smoothe over uneven pavements and cobbles or drop high kerbs, except for complaining to my council. As a witch, activist and poet, I believe words have magical power, and Irish tradition also

---

6 O'Brien, 2020

attests to it, with magic and poetry meeting in Draiocht Ceoil, a "magical tradition of Ireland involving the use of sounds, words". They also meet in the Rosc, appearing "as *roscada* in early Irish law, as battle magic in tracts such as 'Forbuis Druim Damhghaire' ('The Siege of the Ridge of the Stag's Cry') from the *Book of Lismore*, and as deeply mystical poetic magic ('The Call/Challenge of Amergin, the first mortal poem')".[7]

> "*I collect Orthoceras and carry it in my handbag or purse for defence and protection ...*"

For now, being careful where I need to, I am soon in town and heading the few yards to Crystal Cavern Gifts, a gift shop that also sells various Wiccan items: crystals, fossils, incense and herbs for magic, pendants to wear as talismans. As I've become more Irish-focused, so too has my shop-buying. Today I buy four white quartz tumbled stones – white quartz being a crystal found in Ireland's landscape (Newgrange, for example) and lore[8] – and two small orthoceras fossils. Plentiful in Europe but not traditional to Irish practice, I collect Orthoceras and carry it in my handbag or purse for defence and protection, as it reminds me of spearheads, battle and the Morrigan (UPG).

My path has Ireland at its root, not Britain, and I spend most of my time there: by learning about its gods, lore and language, and being accountable to the Irish pagans I know whose living tradition I've made my own. But this demands that I also connect with England, the land I inhabit, in both its beautiful and ugly aspects. Atherstone loudly attests to both. After the witchy shop, I wheel the opposite way toward Atherstone Visitor & Heritage Centre, a small shop-sized museum on the roadside with exhibits and information

7 Moorkens Byrne, 2021
8 Thompson, 2005

about Atherstone, its surrounding villages and the county of
Warwickshire. Many of our shops have high steps into them,
inaccessible for wheelchairs. The heritage centre has a ramp,
so I'm able to go in and ask for a book that the Covid-19
lockdown kept me from, which explores the latest evidence
to lay claim on Mancetter – the next village over, also near
Watling Street – as the site where Boudicca, Brythonic-Celtic
queen of the East Anglian Iceni tribe, fought her final battle
against the Romans.[9] When I first moved here, just prior to
the book's publication, I watched the author, Margaret
Hughes, deliver a talk on the book's research at the library.
I was enthralled. The hope that I might live on a land that
once resisted Roman colonization to defend a Celtic identity
– a land "before all the bullshit happened" (my words, not
hers!) – resonated with my hope as a trans woman, traumatized
by the grief of a once-strong gender identity lost to cis societal
brainwashing, that I might re-connect with my Self "before
all the bullshit". Thankfully they do have the book, so I buy
a copy.

I also buy one containing more detail about Atherstone
itself. It has a nicely "official"-sounding explanation of why our
hat-making – or "hatting" – industry ceased:

> The decline in hat wearing perhaps started with the coming of
> the motor-car, and the lack of the need of weather protection
> when out of doors. The death of the trade however was due to
> the universal trend towards a more informal type of clothing
> which accelerated after the Second World War.[10]

But another explanation I find later bears an uglier truth: one
of the largest markets for the Atherstone hatting industry was
to equip black slaves in the West Indies and America. Slaves
wore a hat called a billycock, which was similar to the kind
of hat that was worn by the British army. It was production

9 Hughes, 2020
10 Austin, 2005

of these hats that helped keep the Atherstone hat trade buoyant ... "I do believe that the Atherstone hat trade suffered a major impact from the abolition of slavery", says local historian and author Judy Vero. "One only has to look at the records for 1833-4, especially the Vestry Minutes for Poor Relief to see the hardship of the time."

I ask whether they have any material on local folklore, especially fairylore, to look at potential consequences of cutting back my bushes. My question is met by shrugs and a recited list of pagan sites further afield. The legend of the Rollright Stones is mentioned, which "straddles the border between Warwickshire and Oxfordshire ... The common people usually call them the Rolle-rick stones and dreameth that they were sometimes men by a wonderful metamorphosis turned into hard stones." *Camden's Britannia*, 1586.[11] But locally most of it's gone, they tell me. Because I'm too unconfident to use the bus alone, and the train station is unstaffed – so I'm likely to get stranded somewhere without help – foraging further afield is more stressful than it's worth. The evening is setting in, and so is physical and mental exhaustion. Time to go back home, where the magic happens, and my cosmology of access can really open up.

LAND, SEA AND SKY

When I'm home I sit down with my second coffee of the day. On my lounge coffee table is a shallow ceramic bowl filled with pebbles, hagstones and Orthoceras fossils representing Land, to the left; blue-dyed gravel representing Sea in the centre; and clear glass beads representing Sky, to the right. "The Celts, even the gods, would swear by the realms of land, sky, and sea. [The Dagda] makes a promise to the three men from whom he obtained his club right after reviving them ... 'Sun and moon, land and sea, provided that I slay my foes with it and bring my friends to life.' Under that condition,

---

11 Edwards, 2021

a lone of the staff was given to him: *How the Dagda Got His Club, Yellow Book of Lecan* (Bergin)".[12] Over coffee, I dedicate myself to these three realms, and drop copper coins from my purse into the bowl as if into a wishing well. When the "wish" represented by a coin feels answered, it goes back in my purse, and out into the world to manifest for someone else (UPG).

I have a long-term plan to make a set of sacred site altars that I could journey to, interact with, give offerings at. "The different Tuatha Dé Danann had their own sacred places and real world sites that belonged to them".[13] My bedside table – four drawers tall – is the perfect place to construct them: four drawers for four sites belonging to four gods: Uaimh na gCat for the Morrigan; the Holy Well at Kildaire for Brigid; Síd in Broga (Newgrange) for the Dagda; and perhaps the Hag of Beara rock, Bhéara, County Cork, for the Cailleach. For now, I place one quartz crystal in each drawer as a place-holder, transfer from my wheelchair onto my bed and spend some time there in meditation and prayer – to the gods and for their sites, the land and its people.

The idea for my sacred site altars came as a result of being in community with O'Brien, whose various online community spaces and teaching materials have formed my "authentic connection", and whose Irish Pagan School has been my túath (in Irish, "tribe", "community", literally "petty kingdom") for a few years now. On journeying, O'Brien writes:

> The full power of this land is at its most potent when felt directly. All of that being said … for some folk, physically being here is just not possible in this lifetime, for a myriad of reasons ranging from disability to economic responsibilities. If that is your situation, don't despair! I have devoted my life to facilitating authentic connection to Ireland, in this world

12 Godwin, 2019
13 Daimler, 2015

or the Other. I urge you to begin a Journeying practice (there are multiple free and paid options on my YouTube Channel and through the Irish Pagan School, as well as regular resources when you join my mailing list community at https://LoraOBrien.ie), and do your best with what you have. It is definitely possible to begin working on a connection from elsewhere, right now.[14]

Given my positionality to Ireland – as a colonizer from a nation that subjected it to centuries of violent occupation, a legacy that still continues – I felt that just as guided journeying should be done by invitation, in right relationship to Ireland and its community, so should these altars. O'Brien describes the technique of creating a journeying site that I'll apply to my model-making:

Get as many pictures and reports of the place you wish to visit as you can find and literally build – over a series of meditations, visualizations, and journeys – the place in your mind. You do this until you can see it all clearly, hold it easily, smell the earth and surroundings, hear the sounds, taste the air and touch every rock and blade of grass.[15]

Tonight, I take a journey from my pillow before I sleep, thankful again to partake in the power to cross land, sea and sky, to the land of my gods, my ancestors, my *tuath*; and thankful to be enabled with the power to build a cosmology of access, in which, when the outside was inaccessible, I "brought the outside in". If I couldn't go to it, I magically brought it to me. We can journey anywhere, O'Brien emphasizes, as long as we have proper respect for the land's boundaries, and as long as we know how to find our way back.

---

14 O'Brien, 2020
15 O'Brien, 2020

ACKNOWLEDGEMENTS

Firstly, *go raibh mile maith agat* (a thousand thank you's) to Lora O'Brien, John O'Sullivan and all teachers and *tuath* at the Irish Pagan School, whose words, wisdom and fellowship I've drawn from for this essay. Thank you also to Geraldine Moorkens Byrne for serving as sensitivity and proofreader in the final stages. *Do déithe duibh* (may your gods be with you all).

BIBLIOGRAPHY

Austin, J D, *Hats, Coal & Bloodshed: A Short History of Atherstone Street Names, the Mining Villages and the Battles of Boudica and Bosworth*, Atherstone: The Friends of Atherstone Heritage, 2005

"Coventry & Warwickshire: links to the slave trade", *BBC*, September 24 2014, http://www.bbc.co.uk/coventry/content/articles/2007/02/16/atherstone_hatting_feature.shtml

Daimler, M, *By Land, Sea, and Sky: Selected Paganized Prayers and Charms from Volumes 1 & 2 of the Carmina Gadelica*, Copyright: Morgan Daimler, 2011

Daimler, M, *Fairies: A Guide to the Celtic Fair Folk*, Moon Books, 2017

Daimler, M, *Pagan Portals – Brigid: Meeting the Celtic Goddess of Poetry, Forge, and Healing Well*, Moon Books, 2016

Daimler, M, *Pagan Portals – Irish Paganism: reconstructing Irish Polytheism*, Moon Books, 2015

Edwards, C, *Warwickshire Folk Tales*, The History Press, 2021

Godwin, C, "Land, Sky, and Sea in Devotional Practice", *Patheos*, 8 January 2019, www.patheos.com/blogs/fromacommonwell/2019/01/land-sky-and-sea-in-devotional-practice/

Hughes, M, *Boudicca at Mancetter: The Latin, The Land, The Logistics*, Atherstone Civic Society, 2020

"National Folklore Collection UCD Digitization Project", *Dúchas.ie*, www.duchas.ie/en

O'Brien, L, *Irish Witchcraft from an Irish Witch*, Second Edition, Eel & Otter Press, 2020

O'Brien, L, *Rathcroghan, A Journey: Authentic Connection to Irish Sacred Sites*, Irish Folklore Series, Eel & Otter Press, 2019

O'Brien, L, *Rathcroghan: Irish Royal Site*, Cruachan Press, 2012

Patterson, R, P*agan Portals – The Cailleach*, Moon Books, 2016

Thompson, Tok, "Clocha Geala/Clocha Uaisle: White Quartz in Irish Tradition', *JSTOR*, 2005, www.jstor.org/stable/20520880

"We can journey anywhere ... as long as we have proper respect for the land's boundaries, and as long as we know how to find our way back"

ABOUT THE
CONTRIBUTORS

IONA LEE

Iona Lee is a writer of poetry and non-fiction, as well as
a performer, musician and illustrator. She has appeared on
radio and television and has read her work in theatres and
on festival stages all over the UK and Europe. Her work has
also been published widely, and her debut poetry pamphlet
was published by Polygon in 2018, being shortlisted for both
a Saboteur and a Saltire award.

JANE CLAIRE BRADLEY

Jane Claire Bradley is a writer, performer, educator and therapist
based in Manchester. Jane writes novels, short stories, essays and
performance poetry, mostly about teenagers, trauma, queerness,
class, magic and the uncanny. Her first novel, *The Summer
Everything Happened* (Hashtag Press, 2022) won the Northern
Debut Award from New Writing North. Jane is the founder
of For Books' Sake, the non-profit dedicated to championing
marginalised writers, and has her own therapy practice, Rebel
Therapy. Find out more at www.janeclairebradley.com

HARRY JOSEPHINE GILES

Harry Josephine Giles is a writer and performer from Orkney,
living in Leith. Their verse novel *Deep Wheel Orcadia* was
published by Picador in October 2021 and was a Poetry Book
Society Winter Selection. Their poetry collections *The Games*
(Out-Spoken Press, 2018) and *Tonguit* (Freight Books 2015)
were between them shortlisted for the Forward Prize for Best
First Collection, the Saltire Prize and the Edwin Morgan
Poetry Award. They have a PhD in Creative Writing from
the University of Stirling. Their show *Drone* debuted in the
Made in Scotland Showcase at the 2019 Edinburgh Fringe
and toured internationally, and their performance *What We*

Owe was picked by the *Guardian*'s "Best-of-the-Fringe" 2013 roundup in the "But Is It Art?" category. Find out more at www.harryjosephine.com

— — — —

LISA MARIE BASILE

Lisa Marie Basile is a poet, essayist, editor and chronic illness awareness advocate living in New York City. She's the founder and creative director of *Luna Luna Magazine* and the creator of Ritual Poetica. She's the author of *The Magical Writing Grimoire*, *Light Magic for Dark Times* and *City Witchery*, as well as a few poetry collections. Her work can be found in *The New York Times*, *Catapult*, *Narratively*, *Refinery 29*, *Bustle*, *Sabat Magazine*, *Cunning Folk*, *Best American Experimental Writing*, *HealthCentral* and more. Follow her @lisamariebasile.

— — — —

STELLA HERVEY BIRRELL

Stella Hervey Birrell is a poet and baby hedge-witch living in Midlothian, Scotland. Her work has been published in various places and her first poetry pamphlet with Algia Press sold out in its first month. She was Tyne & Esk's writer of the year in 2021, and has been awarded the Glasgow Women's Library Bold Types poetry prize.

— — — —

AW EARL

AW Earl has been quietly practicing paganism and reading tarot for longer than they've been doing most other things they care about. A writer, storyteller and performer their work centres queerness, deviant bodies, folklore and the macabre. As Alys Earl, they published the gothic novel *Time's Fool*, and short story collection *Scars on Sound*. They can usually be found lurking on Twitter (@alysdragon), where they are politely angry about transgender issues, or else wandering the Scots Borders and East Anglian coasts.

SABRINA SCOTT

Sabrina Scott has been reading tarot and doing witchcraft for more than twenty years. Their witchcraft practice is deeply intuitive and mediumistic, with a focus on trance, ecstasy and communing with the dead. They see magic as a way of building relationships with non-human beings, and as a way of healing and grounding the body, mind and soul. Sabrina owns a successful spiritual teaching and consulting business, with clientle worldwide. Her online courses and group coaching programs, Tarot Without Bullshit and Magic Without Bullshit, have helped hundreds of students build skills and confidence in their spiritual and divinatory practices. She is the creator of the graphic novel *Witchbody* (Weiser, 2019).

SIMONE KOTVA

Simone Kotva is an academic, writer and student of Nordic folk magic (trolldom). Originally from Sweden, she now teaches philosophy of religion at the Universities of Oslo and Cambridge, and is the author of a book on spiritual exercises and the practice of philosophy, *Effort and Grace: On the Spiritual Exercise of Philosophy* (Bloomsbury, 2020). In 2020–2021 she convened the wildly popular Magic and Ecology symposium.

ABOUT THE CONTRIBUTORS

LILITH DORSEY

Lilith Dorsey M.A. hails from many magickal traditions, including Afro-Caribbean, Celtic and Native American spirituality. Their traditional education focused on Plant Science, Anthropology and Film at the University of R.I, New York University and the University of London, and their magickal training includes numerous initiations in Santeria also known as Lucumi, Haitian Vodoun and New Orleans Voodoo. Lilith Dorsey is a Voodoo Priestess and in that capacity has been doing successful magick since 1991 for patrons, the editor/publisher of *Oshun-African Magickal Quarterly*, filmmaker of the experimental documentary *Bodies of Water :Voodoo Identity and Tranceformation*, choreographer/performer for jazz legend Dr. John's "Night Tripper" Voodoo Show and author of *Voodoo and African Traditional Religion*, *55 Ways to Connect to Goddess*, *The African-American Ritual Cookbook*, *Love Magic*, *Orishas, Goddesses and Voodoo Queens* and *Water Magic*.

ALICE TARBUCK

Dr Alice Tarbuck is an award-winning writer and academic, based in Edinburgh. She has taught Creative Writing at the University of Dundee, and is a Scottish Book Trust New Writer's Awardee for poetry. Her debut non-fiction book *A Spell in the Wild: a year (and six centuries) of Magic* is published by Hodder & Stoughton.

CLAIRE ASKEW

Claire Askew's books include the poetry collections *This Changes Things* and *How To Burn A Woman* (Bloodaxe), the fiction writing guide *Novelista* (John Murray) and the multi-award-winning novel *All The Hidden Truths* (Hodder &

Stoughton). She is a Jessie Kesson Fellow and former Writer in Residence at the University of Edinburgh. She lives in Cumbria.

EM STILL

Em Still is a writer based in Edinburgh, Scotland. Em has taught creative writing at Edinburgh Napier University, was poetry editor for *Malefaction* magazine and has been featured at poetry events around Scotland. Most recently, Em transformed their day job into The Gull's Grocery, a worker's co-operative, grocery store and arts space. They can be found @EmStillWriting.

BRIANA PEGADO

Briana Pegado FRSA is a fellow of the Royal Society of Arts. She is a trained ThetaHealer, a psychic intuitive and a student of astrology. She has written for years on topics ranging from the rise of feminist mysticism for Monstrous Regiment Publishing to rising inequality in the creative industries for Bella Caledonia. She was named one of Scotland's 30 Under 30 Inspiring Young Women in 2017 and has won a number of awards for her work as a social entrepreneur in the creative industries over the last eight years. Currently, she is chair of the board of YWCA Scotland – the Young Women's Movement – an organisation focused on building young women's leadership. She is a data-driven innovation ambassador for the Edinburgh Futures Institute. Follow her on instagram @brianapegado and on Twitter @briana_pegado.

MEGAN RUDDEN

Megan Rudden is a visual artist and writer from Edinburgh with a lifelong interest in the occult. Her ongoing research into the history of witchcraft, mysticism and spirituality has informed much of her interdisciplinary art practice which moves across performance, object making, text and drawing. Megan has performed and exhibited at various locations across the UK and her writing has been published on several platforms since completing postgraduate study in Art Writing at Glasgow School of Art.

MADELYN BURNHOPE

Madelyn Burnhope is a disabled transfeminine writer and Irish-focused pagan witch based in Atherstone, North Warwickshire, UK. Her poetry has appeared widely in journals and anthologies in print and online, most recently *Stairs & Whispers - D/deaf and Disabled Poets Write Back* (Nine Arches Press, 2017). Her debut collection was *Species* (Nine Arches Press, 2014), and she is currently working on a second.

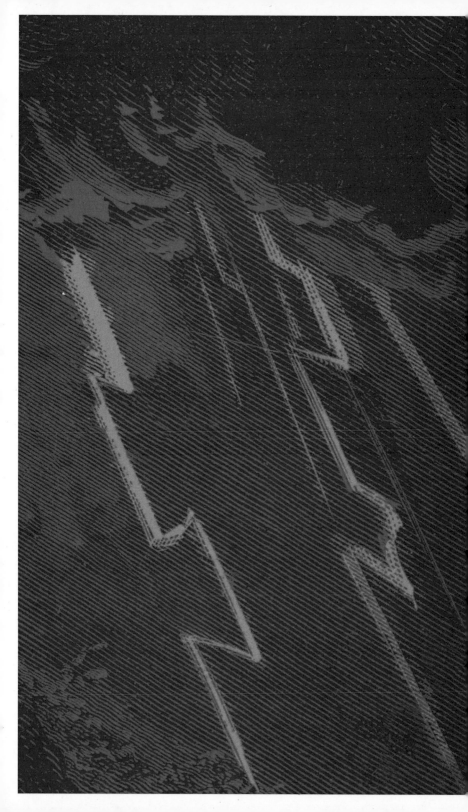

CLAIRE AND ALICE'S ACKNOWLEDGMENTS

Huge thanks are due to our wonderful editor Ella Chappell, who believed in this book back when it was just little more than a vague pitch – Ella, we have so appreciated your support and patience. We'd also like to thank Brittany Willis for her diligent work in polishing up the manuscript, and Jasmine Hromjak and Karen Smith for making such a beautiful finished product. Everyone at Watkins who worked on this book: we thank you.

We'd also like to thank all the contributors who appear in these pages for lending us their words, but also for their endless patience and understanding as, together, we built this book during the most difficult two years that many of us will ever have experienced. A special mention for Stella Hervey Birrell, who stepped in last-minute to fill a sudden space. We'd like to thank Lisa Ellwood for her ideas and her enthusiasm for this project – Lisa, we hope to work with you again in the future.

Endless gratitude goes to our Toil & Trouble students and alumni: thank you, all, for giving us so many opportunities to examine and discuss ideas about witchcraft ethics, theory, and practice. This book is for all of you.